RHINO 2020

*RHINO*: The Poetry Forum, Inc. is
supported in part by grants from the
Illinois Arts Council, a state agency,
Poets & Writers, Inc., and
The MacArthur Funds for Arts & Culture
at The Richard H. Driehaus Foundation.

MacArthur Foundation

DRIEHAUS FOUNDATION

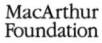

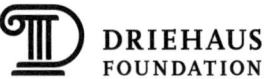

*RHINO* is published annually and considers submissions of poetry, flash fiction/ short-shorts, and translations.
Regular reading period: April 15 to July 31.
Founders' Prize reading period:
September 1 – October 15.

Address all correspondence to:

*RHINO* * P.O. Box 591
Evanston, Illinois 60204
Include SASE
or
editors@rhinopoetry.org

*RHINO* strongly encourages electronic submissions. Consult rhinopoetry.org for details. For those submitting via the postal service, please include an SASE for response.

*RHINO 2020* is available for $16,
plus postage; back issues are also available.
To order, visit our website,
or send check or money order
to the P.O. address.

Our website features *RHINO Reviews*, as well as
excerpts from past and current issues, events, audio
poems, poet interviews, and prize-winning
poems from our annual Editors' Prizes
and Founders' Prize Contest.
(See back cover for details.)
rhinopoetry.org

ISBN: 978-1-945000-04-1
ISSN: 1521-8414

© 2020, *RHINO*: The Poetry Forum, Inc.

All rights to material in this journal revert to
individual authors after *RHINO* publication.

## EDITOR
Ralph Hamilton

## SENIOR EDITORS
Virginia Bell
Angela Narciso Torres

## MANAGING EDITORS
Jan Bottiglieri
David Jones

## ASSOCIATE EDITORS
Darren Angle
Carol Eding
Naoko Fujimoto
Gail Goepfert
Ann Hudson
John McCarthy
Beth McDermott
Elizabeth O'Connell-Thompson
Jacob Saenz
Jessica Terson
Nick Tryling

## OUTREACH EDITORS
Naoko Fujimoto
Taylor Mignon
Kenyatta Rogers

## CONTRACT MANAGER
Rochelle Jones

## WEBMASTER
Darren Angle

## INTERNS
Kathryn Bick
Payton Gosse
Michael O'Rear

## ADVISORY BOARD
Michael Anderson
Laura Cohen
Albert DeGenova
Joanne Diaz
Adam Green
Valerie Wallace

## CREDITS
Design by David Syrek
Illustrations by Naoko Fujimoto
Page number ornament by David Lee Csicsko
Production by Godfrey Carmona

# CONTENTS

| | | |
|---|---|---|
| Editors' Note | x | |
| Editors' Prizes | xii | |
| Founders' Prizes | xiv | |
| **Doha Aboul-Fotouh** | *Begetting* | 1 |
| Jose A. Alcantara | *On the Day His Wife Considers Leaving Him for Another Man, He Weighs His Options* | 6 |
| Li Bai | *In Spring*<br>translated from the Chinese by Michele Baron | 7 |
| Caroline Parkman Barr | *Venus de Milo with Drawers Unto Her Serpent* | 8 |
| Heather Bartlett | *That is Not My Name* | 10 |
| Matsuo Bashō | *#40* | 11 |
| | *#43*<br>translated from the Japanese by Andrew Fitzsimons | 12 |
| Ashwini Bhasi | *Duck* | 13 |
| Bonnie Billet | *The bedroom in Arles* | 15 |
| Jesse Breite | *Abstracted Stood* | 16 |
| Cassandra J. Bruner | *Spinneret Girl before O'Keeffe's Pelvis with the Distance* | 17 |
| Beverly Burch | *Incantation to a Restless Creature* | 18 |
| Catherine Carter | *Ode: Anus* | 19 |
| Kathleen Casey | *Lament* | 21 |
| Luisa Caycedo-Kimura | *Santa Rosa 2015* | 23 |
| Avraham Chalfi | *So What If a Man*<br>translated from the Hebrew by Atar J. Hadari | 27 |
| Susanna Childress | *Baby at the Back of the Refrigerator* | 28 |
| Anthony DiCarlo | *I have never seen anything like this—* | 29 |
| Ruth Dickey | *It's come to this…* | 30 |
| Lisa Dordal | *The Last Time* | 31 |
| Wendy Drexler | *The Galapagos Tortoise* | 32 |
| Dylan Ecker | *Freestyle* | 33 |
| Kelly Egan | *flyer* | 34 |
| Bryce Emley | *Wash* | 35 |
| Kristina Faust | *In a Red Lobster Parking Lot, Grand Rapids, Michigan* | 36 |
| | *We Now Know the Rate at Which the Universe Is Expanding* | 37 |

| | | |
|---:|:---|---:|
| Majda Gama | *Pastoral in the Anthropocene* | 38 |
| Henry Goldkamp | *Yoshida Kogyo Kabushikikaisha* | 39 |
| Mariam Gomaa | *Exolesco* | 42 |
| Beth Gordon | *Tea Leaves and AI* | 44 |
| Peter Grandbois | *The wind is an ocean* | 45 |
| Stuart Greenhouse | *In a Soft November Light* | 46 |
| Robert Hahn | *Life Is Beautiful* | 48 |
| Myronn Hardy | *Mr. Coltrane It's Autumn in these Mountains* | 49 |
| Albe Harlow | *Aniline Dye* | 51 |
| Andrew Hemmert | *Cocktail Theory* | 52 |
| Natalie Homer | *Lion, Lamb, et al.* | 53 |
| T.R. Hummer | *Ohio* | 54 |
| Michael Hurley | *Chatting with Death* | 55 |
| Jade Hurter | *Venus Anadyomenes* | 56 |
| Noriko Ibaragi | *Room* <br> translated from the Japanese by <br> Peter Robinson and Andrew Houwen | 57 |
| Mitsuko Inoue | *proposal* <br> translated from the Japanese by <br> Chikako Nihei and Andrew Houwen | 58 |
| Satoshi Iwai | *Shooting Star* | 59 |
| Devin Koch | *Other Devin* | 60 |
| Michael Lauchlan | *Prevailing* | 61 |
| Kabel Mishka Ligot | *Habeas Corpus* | 62 |
| Amy Gong Liu | *To My Last Thought* | 64 |
| Diane K. Martin | *Signal to Noise Ratio* | 65 |
| Michael Martin | *The First Book I Read After My Mother's Murder Was* In Cold Blood | 66 |
| Chloe Martinez | *The Movement* | 67 |
| Tara McDaniel | *Lucky, Oklahoma* | 68 |
| Cameron McGill | *William Blake & The Eternals* | 70 |
| Jennifer Stewart Miller | *[We Can't] Save Everything* | 71 |
| A. Molotkov | *Complicit in Incompleteness* | 74 |
| Alex Mouw | *Genesis 3* | 75 |
| Marcus Myers | *Our Love is a Delicate Material in a Cornell Box as Vast as the Sea* | 77 |
| Nawal Nader-French | *Mother as text* | 79 |
| Christopher Nelson | *To Certainty* | 80 |

# CONTENTS

| | | |
|---:|---|---:|
| Munir Niazi | Today Too (Ajj Da Din Vee)<br>translated from the Punjabi<br>by Zafar Malik and Faisal Mohyuddin | 81 |
| John A. Nieves | Between Glaciers | 82 |
| Caleb Nolen | Reunion | 83 |
| James Norcliffe | The Museum of Unnatural History | 84 |
| Eric Pankey | The Entrepreneur | 85 |
| M. Nasorri Pavone | How to Motivate a Dog | 86 |
| Marielle Prince | In Order | 88 |
| Charles Rafferty | Asymmetry | 89 |
| Laura Ring | Range of Absence | 90 |
| Linwood Rumney | The Devens Literacy Test: *Do beds run?* | 91 |
| Natasha Sajé | slipskin | 92 |
| Christopher Salerno | Headfirst | 93 |
| Mara Adamitz Scrupe | Nancy's Soliloquy/ Dr Lightfoot's Law of<br>Dynamic Overlap/ Ivy Hill Plantation, 1853 | 95 |
| | thoughts on borders | 98 |
| Maureen Seaton | 4th Stage Metaphoric Breast Cancer | 100 |
| Tsuji Setsuko | Metallic Logic<br>translated from the Japanese<br>by Taylor Mignon and Andrew Houwen | 101 |
| Donna Spruijt-Metz | I need the long march | 102 |
| Seth Stephanz | Secular Liberal Democracy | 103 |
| Lisa Gluskin Stonestreet | Ripe | 105 |
| Marcela Sulak | Genesis | 106 |
| Paige Sullivan | Ascension with Box of Chocolates | 109 |
| Elizabeth Sylvia | Coumadin | 110 |
| Andrew Szilvasy | Snow Day, with Oranges | 111 |
| Shuzo Takiguchi | LINES | 113 |
| | basse élégie [low-down elegy]<br>translated from the Japanese<br>by Mary Jo Bang and Yuki Tanaka | 114 |
| Eric Tran | Hippocampus | 115 |
| Leah Umansky | Tyrant as Self Reflection | 116 |
| Alia Hussain Vancrown | Funeral Home | 118 |
| Hannah VanderHart | My Mother's Brown Plaid Drapes | 119 |
| Anastasia Vassos | the modern poet tries to read<br>Sappho in ancient greek | 121 |

| | | |
|---|---|---|
| **Mark Wagenaar** | *It Was While I Was Looking at the Oldest Wooden Wheel Ever Discovered* | 123 |
| **Claire Wahmanholm** | *Metamorphosis with Milk and Sugar* | 125 |
| **Jessica L. Walsh** | *Blood Gutter* | 127 |
| **Mike White** | *Load-Bearing* | 128 |
| **John Sibley Williams** | *Carcinogen* | 129 |
| **Caitlin Wilson** | *Geyser* | 131 |
| **Shannon K. Winston** | *Notes From the Pantry, 1990* | 133 |
| **Jane Zwart** | *Grief is the gouge* | 136 |
| **Martha Zweig** | *Version of Charlotte* | 138 |

| | |
|---|---|
| Contributors' Notes | 140 |
| Donors | 156 |
| Founders' Prize Information | inside back cover |

# EDITORS' NOTE

2019, our 43rd year, was good to *RHINO Poetry*. Going into 2020, our active local programs—the Poetry Forum, our monthly workshop, and RHINO Reads!, our monthly reading series—continue to thrive, as does *RHINO Reviews*, our monthly online magazine of poetry reviews which has published 22 issues since its inception in 2018. Meanwhile, among the special features to be found in *RHINO 2020* are ten poems in translation, eight from Japanese.

In his book of essays, *Music at Night*, Aldous Huxley wrote: "There is, at least there sometimes seems to be, a certain blessedness lying at the heart of things, a mysterious blessedness, of whose existence occasional accidents or providences (for me, this night is one of them) make us obscurely, or it may be intensely, but always fleetingly, alas, always only for a few brief moments aware."

As Huxley suggests, the expected, the ordinary, the necessary repetition of daily routines, no less than our justifiable worries about health, money, relationships and the more global issues, can render us strangely numb to the potential wonder all around us. Yet it is the uncanny power of poetry to break through the daze of busyness and habit—both to rend and to render—returning the world once again to a place unfamiliar and numinous, luscious and vibrant, contrary and wondrous, and yes, blessed. These moments are, indeed, "fleeting," and yet one breathes them in like fresh, vitalizing air rushing into a long-closed room.

Here are just a few hints of the relish you will encounter within:

You've walked through the open gate of your country
hotel, accompanied by moths & the spectacular
air flowing across the night-damp grass.
It is twilight, yet all the silhouettes make sense:
The hour full of dogs walking their humans.
White hares pause on the edge of dark vision—
they allow your passage & stand still.

**Majda Gama**

My husband is across the aisle
from me, surfing movies, and I'm playing
the same lonely song on repeat, not because
I'm sad, but because something about it
untethers me, lets me submerge in
the hot bath of a mood, memories of past
moments in the dark.

**Paige Sullivan**

                    lizards dart in & out of cracks or lie benumbed amongst
burdock catch-spring/ stickled/ spurred
ovate seeds/ burred bolls while reckless rule-less ghost moths

skim & lek/ scroll & whitecap/ billow & spray      exploding
in quiver-pleasured raves & gullies
                                        **Mara Adamitz Scrupe**


This is not where I meant to be. By the trash carts
two seagulls take turns riding upward on a draft,
a thousand miles from salt water, but cast against the iron sky
they are sailors in sun-bleached whites, sailors in an old port
where the bars are called Copenhagen, Kingston, Rotterdam
                                        **Kristina Faust**


red-plated fish skillfully collide head-on in the intersection
                that's when you hide your face
                            in a fine-tuned gasping
a rose becomes weighty and downcast
                        and the tigress splits
                                        **Shuzo Takiguchi**
                                        translated by Mary Jo Bang & Yuki Tanaka


the night
bows the way everything bows
over its own meal,
loves the way every horse loves
grass between its teeth.

                                        **Anthony DiCarlo**


Join us in exploring the poems of *RHINO 2020*. Breathe. Taste. Feel. Bleed. Laugh. Marvel. Mull. Savor. And find the world anew.

# EDITORS' PRIZES 2020

## FIRST PRIZE

*4th Stage Metaphoric Breast Cancer*
by
Maureen Seaton

## SECOND PRIZE

*Habeas Corpus*
by
Kabel Mishka Ligot

## HONORABLE MENTION

*Santa Rosa 2015*
by
Luisa Caycedo-Kimura

## TRANSLATION PRIZE

*LINES*
by
Shuzo Takiguchi
translated from the Japanese by Mary Jo Bang and Yuki Tanaka

# FOUNDERS' PRIZE 2020

### FIRST PRIZE
*Headfirst*
by
Christopher Salerno

### RUNNERS-UP
*Nancy's Soliloquy/Dr Lightfoot's Law of Dynamic Overlap/Ivy Hill Plantation,1853*
by
Mara Adamitz Scrupe

*Pastoral in the Anthropocene*
by
Majda Gama

In addition, we selected contest poems by the following poets for publication in this issue of RHINO:

| | |
|---|---|
| Catherine Carter | Cameron McGill |
| Kristina Faust | Christopher Nelson |
| Jade Hunter | Caleb Nolen |
| Zafar Malik | John Sibley Williams |
| Michael Martin | |

Information on next year's contest can be found on the inside back cover and at rhinopoetry.org.

Doha Aboul-Fotouh

# Begetting

I grow up thinking Kafra Nafra was
one of the stories my dad would invent.
Like Kalamazoo or the wolves at night
who howl so I hug him tightly after
he turns off the lights. Or that bananas
help when you have a cold. Kafra Nafra
is next to *Zifta* which is funny, *zift*
is a rude word. Kafra Nafra has some
houses, a corner store, many donkeys,
and people who can point you to the house
of my family. It has people who will cook
the nicest meal for you when you're meeting
them for the first time. They are a little
related to you and maybe have your
sister's nose. Kafra Nafra has a girl
your age who asks *Do you know who I am?*
and you don't because you have an awful
grip on family history, though it comes
naturally for your sister, inherited over
games of chess. Kafra Nafra's people accept
my father's Skype calls, indulgences paid
to an older relative. And they say
*we miss you you are important to us,*
which must feel nice from very far away

\* \* \*

/**germ**/ from Middle French /germe/ meaning -egg, bud, seed, fruit, offering-
from Latin /germen/ -spring, offshoot- likely from Proto Indo-European /gen/
-to beget, to bear-. Also, /germane/ meaning to have the same parents
and now to be relevant. But they named the Germans based on neither
or both or the Old Irish word /garim/ -to shout, to be noisy- or

Doha Aboul-Fotouh

the Old Irish word /gair/ -neighbour-, as Arabic /gar/ from
the root g-w-r and meanings -to deviate, to stray, to
persecute, encroach, make inroads-. Then Old Irish
/gair/ from Proto-Celtic /garyo/ shared root for
words in other languages: /gardu/ -groan-,
/geir/ -word-. /garyo/ from Proto Indo-
European /ghehhr/ -to shout, call-
cognate of Greek /gerus/
-voice, speech-.

\*\*\*

meta-
physically
the liver
is known as
the seat
of anger

\*\*\*

A week before he passes away, my dad asks me
in a moment of recognition if I remembered
to brush my teeth.

When I was his kid, he took me to the dentist
(to the grocery store, to the park with the tire swings)
and patted me when I worked myself up to tears,
sat by me the whole time as I had a crown placed.

He talked to the dentist who told him about his son
who died in a motorcycle accident. My dad asked
for that pricy tooth colored composite. The dentist said
why bother over a milk tooth?

\*\*\*

Some people go through and some people —
        I don't know it's just God, the way he does it.

Oh you never know, Mary.
    No you don't.
        He's going to be pooped when
            they take him off of the machine.

Plus they got the two catheters
    draining his lungs.
    It's not a small one, it's a big one.
    One of them he knows the other—
        he don't and if you come in…
    Well, baby, he don't know you now.

And the bowel movement he had this morning…
    Well, there was less blood.

And that's it!

\* \* \*

then they asked me to describe the diseased liver so I wrote:
    it is unremarkable having never seen human liver before. you refused
    the liver I made post diagnosis pre-treatment and cow's liver
    is best marinated in onion juice and fried in ghee. the cancered liver
    becomes symmetric in the body and spreads right to left, tucks itself
    above spleen & both kidneys to protect abdomen from diaphragm and
    that it does this for you. the cirrhotic the cancered the long lived
        liver makes you crazy turns you yellow turns you angry makes you sleep
            in the day and yell at night and sucks all buffers likes cracking bones
                to suck bone marrow that same sound as cracked-bone bone marrow or
                    like water hitting rocks many rocks over and

\* \* \*

maybe it's like the reverse of becoming a butterfly
that all my organs will melt down
but I'll still remember the scent of what I hate.

\* \* \*

Doha Aboul-Fotouh

We curl up as a rat king
on my parent's bed, each of us
tied to a part of my mother,
and all of us crying on her galabaya,
as if we had never agreed *hey
let's not cry on mama,
she has enough.*

She tells me
don't eat your worries
which means
not to carry them with you.

\* \* \*

here is the trick: the roaches can still pass the door.
they pass the door, and make it many minutes or hours
until the poison takes effect, then roll over. i have never
watched one roll over but find them all that way,
in the middle of my home, in the morning or after weeks away.

\* \* \*

I bought bananas
but they've all gone
bad because my dad
is the one who
eats all the bananas.

\* \* \*

I eat the T-bone steaks he bought and placed in the back of the freezer. They're freezer burnt but enough salt and we don't care. I wash dishes with the watered out remains of his dollar store dish soap which does nothing and never did even prior to dilution. I conserve nothing. I have my battery jumped by the mechanic who knew him and replaces my alternator for the price of the part. *I have a very good friend here* he says on the phone to the man with the parts. I brush my teeth with the stockpile of toothpaste he kept in the cabinet above the toilet, and I sleep between the comforter he bought and the mattress he bought but with nobody's palm to pat the blankets down on my sternum when I have a cold.

He took the chest literally. I sit on the furniture he bought and placed. Once, the delivery people took another fork in the road and my father driving behind them cursed and cursed and slept on the ground floor with a baseball bat for a week. We rearrange the living room but nothing jostles out the ghost of him sitting next to the TV and carefully lacing his shoes. I receive his mail and on occasion drive his car and I took his name. I write him down but it doesn't seem fair when he can't say it wasn't like that at all. Rub his beard. Frown.

\*\*\*

I love you and I know that
when you take off your
masks
you will all be
my friends in this life.

You are here?
Who is sleeping upstairs?

\*\*\*

Then days after he died I stand in our kitchen
making harira soup, peeling the chickpeas, when I hear
a single locus of his voice saying *wow-wow-wow.*
By instinct, I work up a sob before I can empty my hands
of the thin chickpea membranes. My mother apologizes
for playing that video. She thinks I am confused,
that I expected to see him across the kitchen island
peering at my progress, wondering when dinner would be.
It was not that. I had not realized how much –

his voice, his swinging tones, his repetitions, his loud
        footsteps downstairs at 5am as he hummed
                      and hummed
                            and hummed.

Jose A. Alcantara

# On the Day His Wife Considers Leaving Him for Another Man, He Weighs His Options

Raven Clan:
    Disarticulating his scapulae, he unfolds his black wings, rises into the bare
    branches of a dead oak, and begins speaking in tongues.

Fish Clan:
    He gashes holes in the sides of his neck, then slides into the deep pool below
    the waterfall where he reflects distorted images of his shimmering scales.

Badger Clan:
    He digs a hole and wiggles, backward, into it. When anything larger than he is
    passes by, he lunges, sinks his teeth into the warm flesh, and grinds
    until bones break.

Moss Clan:
    He wraps himself around a cold, dry stone, hunkers down until he is as thin
    as a wasp's nest, and then waits for a thousand-year storm.

Snake Clan:
    He swallows his own feet, continuing with his legs, arms, body and head,
    until he has turned himself completely inside out, exposing his last true skin.

Sunflower Clan:
    He turns his head, following her path across a darkening sky. When she drops
    over the flat edge of the world, he offers himself to the ravening birds.

Li Bai
translated from the Chinese by Michele Baron

# In Spring

*— from* travels far from the familiar...

reminiscent of spring,
and love,
in whispers of blue-green silk,
slender as grass,
or graceful swallow,
lilting, lyric, in the sky

the mulberry branch,
green,
curves down,
graceful, bending,
and at this moment,
I think fondly of returning home

but, now,
when we no longer know each other,
when my pandered heart is broken,
oh, Breath of Spring,
    ... why enter, now,
between the silken curtains of my bed?

Caroline Parkman Barr

## *Venus de Milo with Drawers* Unto Her Serpent

Call me: long-lost child of Eden

of this wilderness that used to own me—
        first: noon-dazed
    among fields

        I waited for more bodies
          for anything
                interesting—

second: the molder and rust

        a million minutes too many
                    of green—
but then
you passed across my feet
      but then: a beginning

*Come on*, you dare, *be a wild thing*

        No hands to touch you
    so I lick with pomegranate seeds
        still in my teeth

swallow every ancient scale
      you have to offer

            in this strange bed you call
            world

        Wild thing? Yes: something red

Open the drawer—
      fill me with bottled thunder
                      a dozen fish spines
         the hollow sound
    of sin in your mouth—

                    yank me hard
               from this endless summer

    Give me
something else to bite down on

Heather Bartlett

# That is Not My Name
*— after Max Ritvo's "The Hope Chest"*

When I close my eyes there's a brass handle
but in my hand there's only

a bobby pin. I never learned
how to pick locks. How to enter

a room without making a sound.
The sound of stealing is much

like when you say *Darling*
but that is not my name. I only learned

how to turn the deadbolt, to wedge
the board under the knob so the door

couldn't be opened from the outside.
When I close my eyes

someone is knocking. I never learned
how to code switch. The right word

when someone expects return.
How do I let myself

out if the handle will not move?
If the answer is the same

in any language? *Oh
Darling*. That is not my hand.

This is not my mouth. There must be
another word for this.

# Matsuo Bashō
translated from the Japanese by Andrew Fitzsimons

# #40

A pair of deer rub-
bing hair against each other's
hair so hard to please

---

NOTE: meotojika ya / ke ni ke ga soroute / ke mutsukashi
Bashō uses the word *ke* ('hair') three times. *ke mutsukashi* is a pun on *ki mutsukashi* ('fastidious').
Written in autumn of 1671, when Bashō was 28, the poem can be read as an allusion to his love of men.

Matsuo Bashō
translated from the Japanese by Andrew Fitzsimons

# #43

How beautifully
the princess melon reveals
the inner Empress

---

NOTE: **utsukushiki / sono himeuri ya / kisakizane**
*himeuri*: literally, 'princess melon,' *Cucumis melo L. var. makuwa Makino*; *kisakizane*: a play on *sane* the 'core of a fruit' or 'clitoris,' and *kisakigane*, 'empress-to-be.' (Summer, 1671.)

Ashwini Bhasi

# Duck

— *for Jisha*

*According to the National Crime Records Bureau, a crime is committed against a Dalit by a non-Dalit every sixteen minutes.* — Arundhati Roy

I was thinking about you while driving to work this morning
the post-mortem report of 36 wounds, bite marks deep in your bones

screams unheard on a busy street. Evidence lost
or collected too late. They called you *Nirbhaya of the South*,

yet everything about you is different except the iron rod he used.
No night vigils on the streets, lighted candles or songs

of desperate anger for another *India's Daughter*. I was thinking
of you when the duck hit my car. I know

too many witnesses ready to say it was the duck's fault, flying so low
across a busy street, that duck hit car, car did not hit duck — *leaf falls*

*on thorn, thorn falls on leaf, same damage to leaf* — did they hammer this
into us before we bled for the first time or was it after?

No blood was splattered on my windshield slick with rain.
Maybe feathers and flesh lay blended with wilted cherry blossoms

that fell from my neighbor's tree. Did I hear duck bones
crushed on impact? Maybe it was too soft a sound

to penetrate glass. You were landless, living next to a public canal
the news report said your single mother built

## Ashwini Bhasi

the one-room home for you too close to the road. Were you studying
for your law school exam that morning? Did you cook

*Matta* rice for lunch after rinsing red water through the sieve
of your fingers, use palm fronds soaked in kerosene for the wood stove,

did you crush coconut with chilli peppers on a grinding stone? Did you eat
before it happened? How long did it take for you to know

no one was coming? To know, what was happening to you, would be heard
with ears closed like neighbors' doors—steel frames

braced against conscious knowing—I was thinking about you
when I hit the duck? I cursed and swerved, impatiently squirted

wiper fluid to check for damage. The truth is, the relief
from my unsplintered wall of glass pulled me so quickly, away

from the glob of petals or flesh wiped clean from my view,
and the silhouette on the street getting smaller and smaller

in my mirror, was it dead or alive? I did not turn back.
I was already late for my 9 o'clock meeting.

Bonnie Billet

# The bedroom in Arles

I tell my brother I want the corner bed, so he claims it and I sleep under the window.
The summer air fills me with simple expectations: swimming pools, sunshine. The window
opens from the top. I climb up in my flower pajamas and sit with my feet dangling out, watching
the moon and talking to fireflies. A man passes under the window whistling, goes 'round
to the front and rings our bell. He tells my father I'm sitting in the window. Now the beds are in
the center of the room parallel to each other, a dresser sits between them. My father is standing
over me with a belt, my mother watches from the door. The walls and my parents are grey.
I can't remember the beating. The dressers and the walls shimmer, catch fire and burn with
a blue flame. The print of Van Gogh's bedroom in Arles floats above me. He painted five versions
of his bedroom. The one I remember has a red dresser. The walls hold up because my brother and
I believe in walls. My brother, asleep in his bed, is three years younger and never old enough
to understand. For years I woke up every morning and believed it was a new day.

Jesse Breite

# Abstracted Stood

*"and for the time remained stupidly good"*
*— Paradise Lost, Book IX*

Always a pause before the dazzle
after the brink, a blank.
The thing that awes you, stuns you,
plants the wow in your mouth.
Always the space before what comes,
departs. The line is where
you sign your name. Threshold,
your choice. The fruit
you juice—what curls your tongue.
Say what you saw, saw what you can
right down through the eye
of the wood, the pith of the trunk.
But it's lost as soon as you find
the beauty of beauty's invisible
bridges. Call it the wind
that hides you, the breeze
that forgives. Call it the sky blue
sky that proceeds, finishes
through feeling, hinge of
the marvelous—what opens
what closes. Call it the woman's face—
the one you love or the one
you hardly know, that leaves you
dumbstruck, stupid-good
before what happens next.

Cassandra J. Bruner

# Spinneret Girl before O'Keeffe's *Pelvis with the Distance*

Gehenna, I get it. I'm twenty-two, surrounded by glimmering bodies at bars, yet
all I do is yawn black rhododendrons & flakes of calcium. Are these dry heaves why

Gehenna, I long to settle in this sterilized landscape, nap in the primordial
curve of this pelvis? To invite needled light to winnow my own hips? You know

Gehenna, I've studied each misnomer for hell—Hades, Sheol, You—to triangulate
where my departed hang chimes from inverted trees, many of whom

Gehenna, march across your pearlsanded floodplains, uncertain if they can
roost. The murdered & suicides not wanting to be made cypress, rooted. It's funny

Gehenna, how few, if pressed, could read womanhood from these unanswering bones. How us
who remember conjure eidolons, husks of spirit, out of rediscovered letters & plastic necklaces &—

Gehenna, are You the heatswell, the shameflush inflaming my jaw shut & hushed for seasons?
Or are You the memory drawing me toward traces of the boys, girls, children like me
      who spun escape plans and nooses out of their silk?

Gehenna, mid-gallery, I prostrate before you. Let me enter your high deserts. Name me
Jael & pass me a stake under tenebristic light. Please. Before it's too late, raise your dried rosehip—

Gehenna I swear, I see figures cresting the mesa. Though I may once have named You salvation,
Gehenna, I'll tapestry You, my caustic membrane, out, in, & through me yet.

Beverly Burch

# Incantation to a Restless Creature

Just try to make the mind lie down like a good dog.
It barks whenever wind hits the bushes.
It wants a rabbit, a mouthful of flesh in its teeth,
warm scoop of blood. Wants to tangle with the neighbor's
trash, rub its nose in something rotten. Hyped-up
on possibility, it settles for its own tail. Tie a kerchief to its tail,
it runs in circles half an hour. O won't that crazy dog tire?

Squirrels snicker in the poplars, the cat rolls with hilarity.
That slows the poor pooch down. It's why we
keep the cat. Bright notions sift through the blinds.
She stares them down. Isn't she the furry little Buddha,
curled on the silk pillow? Radical non-effort.
Look in her eyes—do you see shame?
She snuffs the foolish mind out, twenty hours a day.

Catherine Carter

# Ode: Anus

Asshole, they call you, lowest and darkest of the low and the dark, butt
of all jokes, mouth of the blast, vent for the Anglo-Saxon
*fart* and *shit*, hidden lip with no tongue:
there are few hymns to you, muscular and grave
and diligent anus, monastery novice faithfully shoveling
soil each day to channel away all we can't use,
simple-lifer, minimalist de-clutterer with more faith
and discipline than Marie or Martha, who also have
anuses.  And though Dante crawled down Satan's haunch
toward a summoner's den of damned friars,
though Absalom kissed Alisoun's nether eye, neither
Dante nor Chaucer praised your keen feeling: neither
your deep exorcisms, your casting-out
of what possesses us so piercing that some have tiled
red pentacles round the base of porcelain toilet pedestals,
arcane stars to fence in what the bowel summons up
and what you, anus, put down, expelling Gothmog,
demon lord of the abyss, in exuberant relief
akin to that of the crow spattering white over newly painted
porch railings—no, nor your power of pain,
rending cramps, unzip-rip of the all-but-healed
fissure reducing even the strong to whimpers,
voiceless endurance of bees who die rather than defile
the hive, desperate anal vents locked tight. Freud
who also had et cetera et cetera thought art was feces
and money was feces but barely praised you,
organ of the creation of space, sacred rat
of black passages where, famously, no sun shines,
much-mocked unloved asshole, living ring
of muscle and nerve splitting wood, carrying water,
his holiness the abbot shitting in the withered field,
Zen of the letting-go, local god at the lintel

Catherine Carter

who opens the way from this second
into the next, the next, each second wholly
and inescapably its own here and now, each one equally holy.

Kathleen Casey

# Lament

The sky folds over like crone skin I am tired of the sky and skin The last flower blooms are not beautiful I am tired of flower blooms The moon's claws start to rise I am tired of the moon's dull claws Tired of the sun's thick furrow Tired of flame plowed orange heat the wind ripping from the south and east in coils and twists      Ants      forage in the kitchen sink I am tired of ants and kitchen sinks and the rugs howling to be cleaned and August's smoke-eyed scent slamming into Fall and sweat splintered under skin and trees smothering with thirst and dust I am tired The famished birds eye a seed   a   worm   the   nectar of blooms and each other I am tired of starving birds and nectar and scrawny worms and shoes waiting to  be  worn  I  am  tired of books begging to be read I am tired of books and sticky worms and careless speech and heat and xanthic smoke The cat rolls on its back I am tired of the cat its snakey spine its sharpened claws its backlit eye I am tired of night and stars

# Kathleen Casey

The earth crawls with wrinkled men and war I am tired of war and turgid men whose reckless words praise slaughter's name Who lie with tiny mouths and white skinned teeth Who always die in peace in sheltered silken sheets I am tired of men and feckless gods and appetites for sacrifice I am tired of terrible beauty and shadows liquefying light The sky folds over like a lid
I am tired

Luisa Caycedo-Kimura

# Santa Rosa 2015

Alongside the creek, eucalyptus
trees loosen their bark,
like unraveling mummies.

Succulents in Courthouse Square
resemble Dr. Seuss characters.

I take pictures of insects
whose names I don't know.

Egrets and herons
in swamps.

Dr. Lee wants pictures
of Hama's chest and back.

\*

Early April, the garden is parched,
like the potatoes we forgot in the oven.

We forget most everything these days.
Anniversaries, birthdays,
wine in the freezer,
Connecticut snow.

\*

Hama's angry that Joe left her
widowed, worries
when I take long on errands,
when my husband coughs.

\*

# Luisa Caycedo-Kimura

At Memorial Hospital, the nurses
go on strike, as do some ER doctors.
A fill-in examines the bruises
from her latest fall.

Dr. Dreamy, we call him—
mustache groomed
wider than his bedside manner.

She's allergic to morphine,
loves flowers, hates insects,
wheelchairs, walkers,
anything that crawls.

Did she lose consciousness?
No. Only weight.

\*

I read about rainforests.
Tell my husband
embryonic tree frogs
can choose when to hatch
to avoid deadly threats.

\*

Hydrations now are a few times a month.
Transfusions every three or four weeks.

She leans back in the chair,
does the Sunday crossword.
My husband and I go to a nearby bar.

\*

At home, I slather cream on her torso,
so the bumps won't itch.

She scrubs in the shower
to expunge them.
Dr. Lee recommends a new drug.

\*

In post-war San Francisco
landlords peered through the windows,
told newlywed Joe and Hama
*We don't rent rooms to Japs.*

\*

Nighttime, early June, she and I dig
through a boxload of pictures,
like a novel we read past curfew.

The Depression in Brooklyn.
Tokyo, the war.
The house they lost
to the bombings.

*Father took the burnt slats
and built us a room.
We all lived there for months.*

\*

A late summer morning.
Bees huddled
in a nest formation
on a pin oak branch.

*Ugh! Ghastly!* Hama clenches my hand.

Next morning, only a few remain
frantically flying over and around.

Days later, a dragonfly perches on a bamboo pole.

## Luisa Caycedo-Kimura

*In Japan, red dragonflies are a sign of fall,*
*she tells me. Pats my arm.*

\*

When I was young, mamá told me,
moths seep from our mouths as we die.

Orange,
brown, black wings

flutter past our tongue. We sigh,
then the body is still.

I search for signs in the closet,
the backyard,
the holes in my t-shirt.

\*

Hama-san, second mother,
if you're well for your birthday,
we'll go to the oyster house,
have Kumamotos. A dozen for each.

\*

Monday morning I awaken
as the crows caw reveille.
They gather like soldiers
on a nearby tree.

Hama's wheezing
and gurgling have stopped.

A half hour later,
we'll hear coos
of collared doves in the yard.

Avraham Chalfi
translated from Hebrew by Atar J. Hadari

# So What If a Man

So what if a man
Is a little tipsy
And has nothing at all
Up his sleeve
But sings to himself
As he walks in the street and sings
And sees folk
On their faces carved signs
Of loneliness
But he walks in the street and sings
And sees kids
And heaven
And a tree, another tree
And isn't even relentlessly happy
Or who knows even how much –
Just something inside him sings
So he sings

And gets a little bit lost
Along with all the rest.

Susanna Childress

# Baby at the Back of the Refrigerator

This day, in truth, is like every other. I hold onto my elbows, swat at flies, feed my living children carrots and hummus, berries from the back yard, figs. But I see you there at the far edge of the fridge, undiscernible, your ten weeks of growth fallen, gathered, now sealed into Tupperware, waiting tests our insurance will not, after all, cover: you are only my second dead baby. In truth, we're each in this, together, alone, some summertime caw, mewl, waiver, stump. The neighbor kneels to weed. The dogs curl towards their tails and nap. Is it possible, where you are, to hear your brothers clamoring for kite string, for baubles? Where you are, not only my second dead baby, not the back of the fridge huddled in root-red "products of conception" but the other world, or worlds, the ones we're promised, or perhaps just those we dream of. Maybe it's the same squint-bright, the same soporific green? Ju-ly, Ju-ly. Surely the breeze's sweet lift-and-tilt, a pebble, pocketed, gone through the wash, a friend's red wagon full of little girls, drywall, muffled Blackcats, another ocher butterfly, the cut through a ripe cantaloupe—none of it would hurt so much. I promise myself, when I'm able, not to hold onto finding you one day—that bullshit re: God needing another angel—but to forsake the way I pretend to let you go. See, T? Where you are. Our fingers miss the cold. Our bodies foam at the lake's edge.

Anthony DiCarlo

# I have never seen anything like this—

there are horses in the dark
heads bend low
mouths open
close
to perfection
a warm place for small things and someone
is telling me to go home.

the night
bows the way everything bows
over its own meal,
loves the way every horse loves
grass between its teeth.

# Ruth Dickey

# It's come to this...

It's come to this: my counter filled with scratch-off tickets,
because every path to winning I imagine is closed.

I think of the smell of pencil shavings, endless turning,
getting smaller and sharper all at once. I envy the pencil;

I envy the sharpener. My dad calls the lottery
*a tax on people bad at math*, but I think it's a tax

on hunger sharpened. I talk with friends about courage.
Everyone has a different theory. Everyone gets a poet

or parrot to sit on their shoulders. My mom grew up
in Panama, and had a monkey for a pet. It once peed

on her hair when she was lying on the floor, talking
on the phone. The lesson my grandmother extracted

is this: Don't lie on the phone or talk on the floor,
never turn your back on a monkey. Sometimes we drive

all night, trading off and guzzling cheap gas station coffee till
we can't drive anymore and park, snoozing by dumpsters.

Sometimes the highway is closed. I grab a nickel
from the change jar. Scratch itches unarticulated,

itches forgotten. I wager $40, win $70. Not enough
to matter. I surrender to seven more chances

for sweetness, seven more possible nows. Wish me
luck. Wish me an absence of monkeys.

Lisa Dordal

# The Last Time

The last time I saw my mother,
she was sitting in the front passenger seat

of my father's car. I looked down into her face
through the open window. She looked up at me

and smiled, said hello. Her right hand
resting on the door. She looked older

than her age, but beautiful.
And luminous. Something in her

already beginning to change. Like a seed,
buried in the ground, sensing the sun's

fuller light. She smiled, said hello.
Or maybe I was the seed, she the light.

*I'm here*, she said. And *here* was someplace else.

Wendy Drexler

# The Galapagos Tortoise

You can walk right up to them in the open-
hearted everywhere. They sleep together
in shallow scrapes, extend their necks
to invite finches to nip ticks from the folds
of their skin. So tame, it took just two meat-starved men
from a merchant or whaling or pirate ship
to roll each tortoise over, lash the legs together,
sling them on long poles, carry them back
to the ship, hundreds in a single day, stacked
upside down on their backs so they couldn't
turn over. They could live like that for a year
without food or water. Fresh meat, roasted right
in the shell. The ones not eaten were sold on shore,
their plates separated, boiled and flattened
for knitting needles, bangles, and the comb—
reddish-brown flames that caught the light—
my grandmother wore in her hair.

Dylan Ecker

# Freestyle

Given the average
circumference of a yo-yo,
its whistling rotundness
like a satellite splitting
the sky, its transaxle
a balance beam with two plastic bodies
spooling, its gentle and focused sleep,
you might think the way to maximize sexiness
would be throwing down a cat's cradle
while on the second date
then casually letting slip the fact that
you are the actual president
of the International Yo-Yo Collective
whose only law is the law of love
which commands new bearings
when things get sticky, sympathy
on days when walking the dog just
isn't possible and you know what
he's sick of doing it again and
again, unwinding the kinks
as if his life is one thin pull-string
as if the only direction is down but
goddammit he wants to shoot the moon,
break the solar gravitational field and dissolve
into the aurora of expanding dark, always
reaching further, always
coming back.

Kelly Egan

# flyer

Say a woman has gone missing.
Flyers hold her place

on phone poles, in cafes,
a repeating decimal.

One, two, three, who notices
white noise, far island
of archipelago—

Is she the deity of outposts?


Her attributes: driftwood, dial tone,
flickers in and out of flesh and bone—

Is she out there in a desiccated dress with the desiccated forms?

Is that the ghost of her pinned to public poles,
smeared in rain, and is it hers
whose house I am in when I am drawn

to the peninsula—

Bryce Emley

# Wash

mother how do we follow the ones who brought us here when they go do we speak when we're all that's left to do their speaking mother they said there was fluid on your lungs the tubes were umbilical cords breathing for you do you remember how you pulled them when you came to mother when you breathed it sounded like water do you remember when I floated away in a riptide on a plastic blowup raft that looked like a chocolate doughnut I thought I would be the first of us to drown mother most of the time I'm ok with being wrong do you remember how I slept beside you in a faux leather chair when I moved it sounded like the blowup chocolate doughnut raft did you know I didn't sleep that night mother did you notice the big-bearded nurse looked out of place like when the moon haunts the sky in the day it was sunny on the day you left I remember there were oranges on the ground outside it was Florida still I thought I'd remember much better do you remember that day at the beach a bee landed on my arm I was still enough I could have been glass I could feel the wind from its wings when it left I didn't know such delicate things could be felt even now I feel it in the hairs on my arm did you know that the ocean is swallowing the coasts mother I don't know if you believed it it's ok we didn't fear the same things America has gone to shit without you every son doesn't live to see his mother die I must be grateful you became so small and delicate mother I thought your own breath would break you do you remember how immense it felt how easy did you feel it when you left so delicately mother the leaving so lightly pushing away

Kristina Faust

# In a Red Lobster Parking Lot, Grand Rapids, Michigan

I'll say it was the storm that stopped me
midway to wherever I was going,
but there was also Glen Campbell
on the radio, his Lineman hearing me
in the whine, and those violins, decades back
in a refrigerated studio, letting snow and strain
pass under their fingers into recorded sound.
This is not where I meant to be. By the trash carts
two seagulls take turns riding upward on a draft,
a thousand miles from salt water, but cast against the iron sky
they are sailors in sun-bleached whites, sailors in an old port
where the bars are called Copenhagen, Kingston, Rotterdam,
so each man can sort himself by origin, knowing
through some bone-deep song, this is the place.

Kristina Faust

# We Now Know the Rate at Which the Universe Is Expanding
### — *Expert Says It Will Grow Larger and Colder and Lonelier Before It Ends*

At the diffuse edge I float wrapped in efficient gel
like an ancient in eiderdown, a more poetic insulator for sure
but prone to clumping and a poor filter for the light of dying stars.
Who through feathers could feel the indicating ping of a nearby life?
I've never seen the image of an eider, nor do I know its signal.
If it made a song, how would it be carried, and to what receptacle?
Now music is pure, tuneless legato, one tone pouring into another, no gap, no void, no space between.
It's all we ever wanted, for one note to continue ringing as the next begins.
World without end, as they used to say. Amen, amen.
We've solved space and time. Where did we meet last night?
Everywhere. On that street. In a room. Nowhere.
Long ago in fall we'd get a sense of dying from the low tremolo of insects
like an orchestra under a *subito* hush
waiting for a soloist who never takes her cue.

Majda Gama

## Pastoral in the Anthropocene

You've walked through the open gate of your country
hotel, accompanied by moths & the spectacular
air flowing across the night-damp grass.
It is twilight, yet all the silhouettes make sense:
The hour full of dogs walking with their humans.
White hares pause on the edge of dark vision—
they allow your passage & stand still. You thank them
for not seeing you as predator, as stoat, fox, or kite.
Across the road is a field felled of a tree.
Crows still flock to its absence for shelter
in the indistinguishable night. The quiet
they sit with is the quiet of a world stripped
of its old gods. That the world should end like this.

Henry Goldkamp

# Yoshida Kogyo Kabushikikaisha

*"No one prospers without rendering benefit to others."*

—Tadao Yoshida, The 'Cycle of Goodness' philosophy

*1 Mississippi*

Eating parking lot fish with whatsherface, the janitor. Ablutions goo out the window unit of the church. She chews standing. She lets drip her pickle spit. I swallow the bones out loud.

*2 Mississippi*

She tells me her favorite apple is gala, that she didn't even know that meant party til her 30s.
I tell her if there's one thing man is good at, it's devouring the party between their sweet teeth.

*3 Mississippi*

She tells me an iffy record of a man who committed suicide by cyanide.
He swallowed hundreds of apple seeds, each containing small amounts of the toxic salt.

*4 Mississippi*

Her seedtime was the kind of white pride wandering south county mall
in shrimping boots. You unlearn something new every day.

*5 Mississippi*

Rattle of Busch in the bed of her man's Cheyenne gauges
how fast we go—the speedometer shot, the streets on fire.

# Henry Goldkamp

*6 Mississippi*

I like the gold parts of her teeth, the funny smell of her hands after Brasso-ing the knob of our church too long. I like her punchline in the one where the Cadillac can't swim.

*7 Mississippi*

A picnic of brown apples listens the sliding brown water. Her stye eye sings ugly.

*8 Mississippi*

Can you get my back. A wink. Hundreds of gulls flood us, yelling, egging us on. She ashes in a bottlecap. I got her back. There is no sun in sight.

*9 Mississippi*

If a man savors the flesh of paradise that many times and still wants to go through with it, he deserves to die.

*10 Mississippi*

She takes my lips like a lollipop of grease. A barge ruts against monster truck tires, alone. Sand is falling to the bottom of her coffee cup. We gonna fuck the animals right back onto that ark.

*11 Mississippi*

Telephone wire strung across the twilight—a giant cat's cradle. I nurse her cocktail of denim lemonade. Sugar ants in route, singing the invisible.

*12 Mississippi*

She asks to be spanked a little. *Honey can we park it out back and have a party in your pink Cadillac?* Softly belting.

*13 Mississippi*

YKK is tattooed on the tip of her thumb, so many times has she unzipped to *Fire*, or *I'm on fire*, or *Streets of fire*. She puts herself out in the river.

*14 Mississippi*

Deeper, in the loom of giant night, babies play Marco Polo in the black squish. Her pockmarks a constellation of crusty stars.

*15 Mississippi*

The mud suckles our toes. Pollen floats us hot snow.
The moon blinks its pink eye.

Mariam Gomaa

# Exolesco

*an immigrant's elegy
in seven parts*

1//
the word caravan was invented for my people:
pilgrims traveling across the desert
of North Africa or Asia.

>
> 2//
> a caravan travels 3000 miles;
> a fraction becomes this America:
>
> at one border there is a library that lives in two countries,
> a row of potted plants delineates one country from the other
> on this shared continent;
>
> > at the other border there is a proverbial wall,
> > promised, unseen, pending.

3//
my first country straddles two continents,
my second, two states of being.

> I drink my old country distilled,
> its essence absorbed and served as all-American things
> I would not have known to love.

> in the purple lip of democracy, I am always fed
> only to go hungry for a seat at the table.

       4//
       I am told a body with two countries cannot exist.
       how will I explain to my ancestors—
       the first part of a person's erasure is looking away.

       I busy myself collecting beautiful objects;
       there are too many beautiful things to keep.

   5//
   light from the nearest star takes four years to reach us;
   I believe in the power of a small adjustment
   in the time it takes for a light to bloom.

       there are 365 ways for an immigrant to disappear;
       I am haunted every day of every year.

6//
we converge at the library,
a body in two countries.

  if I stay here,
  they will always know how to find you.

    7//
    there is an elegant way to end forgiveness:
    in the ripe orange light, we divide our anger like slices of fruit.

       we erase my name from the ledger,
       no one blinks; my brown body fades.

    in the ruthless part of our heart
    I feel safe.

Beth Gordon

# Tea Leaves and AI

There are no deliberate clocks inside   my house, ornate hands pointing to numbers,
eleven as eggs benedict or were   wolf moors depending on your allegiance,
A or P M, the television keeps   track behind its two-way screen, flashing midnight in fluorescent green like it's 19   79, which it might be, I don't
know, my coffee maker knows, I never   re-adjusted its hours according
to daylight savings, fearful of pressing   any button other than brew, my need
for bleak bitter liquid on my slow tongue   so great I dare not question the machine,

my microwave also stores some record   of changing tides, the angry moon, dying
eggs trapped inside my muted ovaries,   my cell phone and computer both insist
I walk the plank, eyes forward, ignoring   the pelicans who live in an endless
oval of dive and swallow, loud shrinking   shadows on my deck, the way squirrels grow fat
or die on the pine needle nest, buzzards   on the highways edge as large as newborn
crones, brake lights like the blood trail my father   left two nights ago when he walked,

dreaming,

into an edge, returned to my mother   in their 67-year-old bed, said

*I feel so lost*, like me he can't recite   the date without a question mark falling
from his mouth, and I mark the passing days   with the maps he drew for me when I could
not translate inches into miles, photos   of our last road trip, evidence that he
once owned our journey, my receding gum   line, the decayed state of each remaining
tooth, soft needlepoint of skin, dead lovers   who never knock on my door, the silence
that wakes me, crying for time, tornadoes,   cold babies, red sirens, trains, the yardstick
on my parent's cellar floor that measures   their backwards growth into the hungry mud.

Peter Grandbois

# The wind is an ocean

*"Once I was beautiful.
Now I am myself."*
—Anne Sexton (1928-1974)

Once, I was an eye
That looked toward
Morning's cry,

An ear breaking
Across evening's
Orange dissolve.

Now, I'm a mouth
Curled with earthworms,
Like murmurings
Over a castle wall.

I'm tempted to close
My body to this dream,
A deposed king
Seeking retribution.

Then, my son tornados
Through the house
Sucking up cookies,
The cat, a throw rug,

And I remember,
I, too, was once a boy
Feeding the other pool,

That empty self,
Whose only rule
Is to open, asking
To be filled.

Stuart Greenhouse

# In a Soft November Light

If we think light is simple — and it is,
there are no light molecules, light DNA strands,
light has no moods, preferences, prejudices,
light can be kept in a cage next to the civets
and not worry its fur off in senseless agitation,
lab tests run on light won't violate ethical standards,
it does not prefer the taste of live flesh
at feeding time, if you come home late
from another hard day at the lab
it will not be standing in a passive-aggressive posture
waiting for you to admit you only stayed late to hurt light
for what it said yesterday which it doesn't even remember
because its mind is always flitting and the new medication
makes every thought a yell and who can think straight,
light is yelling now, almost crying,
is making you feel like you're in
a mid-20th-century novel about how unknowable
the beloved is, how there's always a breaking point
to the complexity of the heart, and we live breaking it,
with all of this yelling, and you say it's ok, it's ok
because you don't want light to come close enough to smell
the cigarette smoke on your clothes, the penumbral cologne —
if light is simplicity itself, and it is
an elemental particle, which means you can't make
anything of it but it itself, still,
did you know it chooses
not just its destination but its path
before it leaves
wherever it shines from?
How does that make sense?

Feynman understood, he drew pages of diagrams
to explain this most basic of phenomena,
calculus and equations smarter than I am, made a career out of his love
for explaining that mystery
is not a matter of endless
recombination,
but of meaning undone
by the sound of its own alphabet
chanting itself weightless in outward devotion,
building no words.

Robert Hahn

# Life Is Beautiful

We had amassed a Ponzi-trove of private jokes.
The gangster's last words in *Little Caesar*—
*Mother of God can this be the end of Little Rico?*—transposed
For your pet name, *Can this be the end of Little Nico?*

Good for a laugh, if you were sick or something, until it wasn't.
I liked to say, anything could be funny except
The Holocaust and being flayed alive.
No, wait, I've got another one.

So your body's been wrecked by septic shock
And I say to this nurse, taking care of business,
Hey, she's an organ donor! So responsible! Does a double take.
*These* organs? Are you kidding me?

No, but wait, remember Benigni's Holocaust film, *La Vita E' Bella?*
Life *Is* Beautiful: wasn't that his debatable point?
"Somewhere, Starbuck, they are making hay in the Andes,"
You loved that one, somewhere people are still reading Melville,

The world is still tragic, still hilarious.
A year after you died, Trump became President.
No, I couldn't believe it either. On election night I slept
At our son's house and was heading for bed when he said,

"Aside from that, it's been a great year."
Remember we used to say, *Mencken would love this?*
He would. If he were alive today, Mencken would still
Be laughing his head off, and still drinking himself to death.

Myronn Hardy

# Mr. Coltrane It's Autumn in these Mountains

But the black cat stares aureate from the drying catalpa.
The remaining leaves are nets unable to hold

what they were.  Preservation     experience
induced mincing what used to be mighty     what

used to lark at weakness.
But you can't hold that self     its

purity     sumptuousness no longer.
You see a black coat.  Someone

is wearing a black
coat as his indigo-eyed dog

rolls in collapsing leaves.
In that air     something

is overripe.  Something is dying.
You can't hold that self

in these mountains.
The rough-rough of them as you

transfigure inside a song.  As you praise
what you have found.

*Glory to its grace.*
*Glory to its grace.*

# Myronn Hardy

You see it in hands    on
thistles flowering mauve.

The gold earth    that
gold in you is a dog barking.

It needs to run.
It needs to roll in collapsing leaves.

Albe Harlow

# Aniline Dye

who
knew
the violence

Leopardi
　not only
picked

the heads
but counted them
　　counted them

as they colored
　magenta
my garden

Andrew Hemmert

# Cocktail Theory

All month I have used
a parking ticket
as a bookmark,
and so my place
is finally defined
by mistake and what I owe.
Against the wishes
of my wallet
I bought another bottle
of bourbon
and so the South
is in my glass again.
Cocktail names are ridiculous
and immortal—
suffering bastard,
hurricane, pain
killer—and the way
my vision narrows
is a window
into the future.
Which is to say, a glass
is a door. A cocktail
is a country after war.

Natalie Homer

# Lion, Lamb, et al.

Wild daffodils wake the winter-weary woods.
On the phone, my father's voice is a tremor
through a thawing pond.

Mild snow, all the bite bred out of it,
falls outside the office window.
Its silence gives it away.

I left the birdfeeder,
shaped like a little house,
empty all winter. My mind, likewise.

Each day I look for the coyote
in the same spot off the highway
but have never seen him since.

T. R. Hummer

# Ohio

It's evolutionarily incorrect to worry about the serpent
  hissing in the winter sawgrass underneath the wind.
Its body twists across a quarter mile of an ancient meteor crater.
  I have strolled the distance of its earthwork spine,
Stood beside its enormous head and lived. Nobody knows
  who sweated here a thousand years ago, hefting earth
In baskets, sculpting this meander. The gods who demanded it
  no longer have names, though they still crawl on its belly
In the deep undergrowth of the oversoul. They are all dead now
  of strange godly cancers, obsidian knives in the gut, oblivion.
It's November in mid-Ohio and rain keeps forgetting to appear.
  The office buildings of Cleveland and Toledo groan
Under the weight of arcane texts. But here the serpent points
  to the equinox in silence on the outskirts of Peebles,
A town that was born with the Cincinnati and Eastern Railway,
  the great iron rattler that ate the otherworldly heart
Of the stone a child in the sky hurled through the head of an eagle
  with a snake in its talons. So much that is not rain has fallen here.

Michael Hurley

# Chatting with Death

He is thin. Gaunt. Asks the time. He offers a cigarette,
lights his own, holds it between his teeth. He screws off each
of his fingertips, one at a time, and places them in a row
on the table, biggest to smallest. Then the knuckles,
then the knuckles after that in separate rows.
Some of them squeak. He sits back and folds his palms.

Says: *Okay then. Let's pretend you're in charge.*

Jade Hurter

# Venus Anadyomenes

You were always a freak, half of you girl, half
who knows what. Smelled of raw oyster or sour
cream. Alone in the bathtub biting your nails.
        Now you drag your body

across the shore, a girlish pulp. Your core
empties, perishable entrails. Your molars
fall out from the roots, cavities like seeds. You
        re-form, pile of salt

poured from shaker, forgetting those last paltry
mornings on land. A new horror calcifies
in the ribcage, adamantine snaking where
        your muscles should be.

A promise of immortality. White scales
on your eyelids. False blood in your cheeks, apple-
bright. Lust blossoms. Your hunger shakes urchins
        from sea beds, filling

your hands with needles. The townsfolk will call you
demon. Will try to thrust knives inside you, but
they will learn. Your last chance to beg for mercy
        in a known language

was to scream. Now when you open your mouth, they
will get on their knees. Your pearly afterbirth
turns foam in the sea. Your spit calcifies, hard,
        golden currency.

Noriko Ibaragi
translated from the Japanese by Peter Robinson and Andrew Houwen

# Room

Bare writing table,
wooden bed-frame,
a spinning wheel –
just these things on the floor;

with stretched plant fibre
a pair of chairs
were lightly
hung on the wall;

of all those I've seen,
this the most beautiful,
not one thing unneeded –
that country's Quaker room.

My desire
is simple existence,
simple words,
a simple life.

Still now, supported,
two chairs lightly floating;
only the deep air
offered me a seat.

Mitsuko Inoue
translated from the Japanese by Chikako Nihei and Andrew Houwen

## proposal

the boy
took his brush out of his parted hair
and brushed the dust off his shoulders

now     he's proposing

listening to it
the shirt-stripes burst out laughing

Satoshi Iwai

# Shooting Star

Take a look at that girl wearing a cadmium-red miniskirt and standing on the mound of ashes. She had been working twenty hours a day for the sushi restaurant which was burnt down last night. The fire chief announced that the cause of the fire was unknown. The restaurant manager was horribly incinerated, but the girl was found entirely unhurt. Now, she serves sushi by herself trotting in the ruins. All you can do is order a special tentacle combo: raw tentacle, poached tentacle, marinade tentacle, and unknown tentacle. She brings them from nowhere to you with a dazzling smile. All you can do is eat them up with no doubt. If you find a tiny cadmium-red star in the bowl of miso soup, give a smile back to her. She will look up at the sky and make a wish in a low voice: *let him burn, let him burn, let him burn.*

Devin Koch

# Other Devin

Other Devin is knocking at my door. It's that time in the afternoon. He doesn't read the *Do Not Disturb* sign I've placed outside. Other Devin is the ghost of my unlived past. He wants me to confront the skeletons in my closet head on. He wants to give me the strength to get rid of them. I can't sleep at night knowing he'll be back tomorrow and again the day after. Other Devin isn't a practicing Jehovah's Witness. He *is* a Jehovah's Witness. Other Devin is the reason why his mom doesn't drink. She can rest sober knowing she's not a failure. Other Devin will make it past Judgment Day and my mom will too. Other Devin is the reason why my parents still sleep in the same bed. He's met every expectation they've set before him. Other Devin is knocking. His wife is standing next to him. There's no need to pray the gay away. Other Devin doesn't pray. He *talks* to Jehovah. He has nothing to hide. Other Devin wants to tell me that Armageddon is knocking at my door, too. But I won't answer that either. Other Devin won't leave. He knows I'm inside. He won't stop looking through the cracks of my blinds. I don't want to meet Other Devin face to face. He'll see the bags under my eyes from keeping myself awake. I'm afraid of dying in my sleep. Other Devin doesn't dream. He doesn't have nightmares.

Michael Lauchlan

# Prevailing

from a distance they seem human
a man no      a woman       her head
leaning to the right     a hat
with tassels hanging    a hand
waving shyly    slyly    or reaching
trembling      grey brown     backlit
at the end of a road    Is she calling
pleading        no     two women
standing close         sisters or lovers
whispering     one into the other's ear
conspiratorial         or only tall
silvergrasses     my wife
couldn't bear to cut back
before the frost       all the blooms
bending in unison to the east

Kabel Mishka Ligot

# Habeas Corpus

*MANILA, Philippines – Former president Ferdinand Marcos can now be buried at the Libingan ng mga Bayani (Heroes' Cemetery). The Supreme Court (SC) on Tuesday, November 8 [2016], cleared all legal obstacles to a Marcos burial, for decades an issue that has driven a deep wedge in Philippine political life. By a vote of 9-5, the High Court rejected petitions that sought to stop the burial of the late dictator.*

dear cadaver,

      i know that it is impossible     to find a word
          for the absence of the body.
only the body itself     communing, as you used to
      with simple folk; but now with the grass,        field
         mice, snakes, in the foothills of quezon
province or perhaps      a river in camarines norte,

        somewhere

      there. now     another body is moving
    south, to be buried        again, crowned in wax
      flowers. stiffly this body lies
    in a refrigerated van. its living     counterparts:
the widow,      lithic; son almost monumental.
        dear corpse, how enviable     their privilege,
   the ability    to say that the body is

     here.

    no fabricated decorations     weigh your soul
down, dear   carcass. consider yourself    blessed
    even after    the spirit passes through
the decomposed body, to be   with the wind, to go
      where the people can say, can see where
   the body is, where    the body is not. dear vessel,

           move

your unhinging      jaw, tattered tongue. speak
        of the time    the remains
of your flesh could not  nourish
          even the ants      starving the sugar
      fields of negros occidental, dearest    disappearing.

Amy Gong Liu

## To My Last Thought

I wish I could

    (comb my fantasies out
    like lice from the dead,)

shake you *so* —

    (violently, so that the stars
    would roll back into the dark)

Diane K. Martin

# Signal to Noise Ratio

Do you remember the *ping-ping-ping* of the radiator
warming, how it sped toward climax, then slowed to
a kind of peace? Now friends, family, and celebrated

icons you thought would always be here disappear.
Their coffins sink into the earth or slip into fire;
their remains remain on Facebook, YouTube, and

documentaries on TV. In California, you can opt for
tree burial, your corpse becoming compost to feed
the tree's roots. In Greece a man gone forty years

was found in a cave, a fig tree rooted in his stomach.
Were you told as a child the cherry pit you swallowed
would sprout? Did you think your mother ate

a watermelon before she had your sister? Some faiths
hold that when you die the spirit returns where
it came from, like a film rewinding, the shooting star's

arc rising back to the Milky Way, or like the fireflies
you caught and collected in jars on summer nights
and released back into the darkness at bedtime.

Michael Martin

## The First Book I Read After My Mother's Murder Was *In Cold Blood*

I'm down in the basement
keeping company with cartons of old paperbacks
manilla envelopes stuffed with photographs and letters
cold bottles of beer inside a fridge.

Upstairs, the harvest is in and the circus is back in town.


I suddenly remember being a boy
and throwing oranges at the train cars
that carried the elephants and lions away
                                        and the circus moved on

Someone wrote that grief would be easier if life were less beautiful

Here's a picture of me under some helicopter blades…

Chloe Martinez

# The Movement

*"To human observers, the painted ladies move with speed and intention,
as if they have somewhere to be. They can fly as fast as 25 miles per hour."*
— "Mass Migration of Painted Lady Butterflies Entrances Californians,"
The New York Times, March 17, 2019

The painted ladies come through moving
in waves, little fluttering rivulets cutting
through the river delta of the sky, not a cloud, not exactly

a shadow, not a straight line among them and yet
a definite direction. You stand in the middle
of the space between buildings, your takeaway

lunch container in one hand and in the other, the idea
of progress, the temporary understanding
that there could be a distinct and also unified

movement towards. The sky is an electric
shade of blue. The truth is, they won't make it.
Not all, not the whole way—so along the route

they lay eggs, lay down, end.
Hatching later, new beings pick up
an invisible thread and just

continue, as if their parents' deaths were a mere
rest stop along the way.
Which, apparently, they were. Don't

cry: you are at your place of employment.
Make your way to privacy. Because you are
human, only there may you be moved.

Tara McDaniel

# Lucky, Oklahoma

You take the shade the dog
found first. His left rear leg
shakes all the time now,

ever since last summer when it was
ground into the gravel
grandpa shoveled before he died.

The golden-eyed pit bull
decided to chase
the garbage truck

and got trapped beneath
its giant wheel
where it rolled over

his hind then his skull. Lucky:
though his hip got mashed,
his head remained mostly

intact. A miracle.
He sticks his back leg
in the air as he bumps

down the front porch
to find a spot
where he can take it easy

somewhere out
in the scrub-grass.
He likes to watch the horses

get watered by
the cattail-sucking neighbor
who slouches back

out from the sun against
the slats of the roadside fence.
In the cool shade

you remember bits of last night's
dream: blown out to sea,
beyond the breakers,

you gathered old diapers, black
plastic bags, spoons, milk jugs,
shampoo bottles and deflated

balloons in order to fashion a raft
that you clutched at and rode in a panic
toward shore. You woke

before you made it back.
On the porch,
tiny tan seed pods

like lucent parchment
lodge in your sandal straps
and the newborn ants

almost translucent
brim from the sparse grass.
Watching how the leaves

of the linden drop over
the maimed orange dog,
you still feel out to sea.

Cameron McGill

# William Blake & The Eternals

*— after Van*

I was a late arrival here.
Years spent pulling my voice apart
like a wishbone for song. I started a band
to meet girls and metaphysicians.
We called ourselves William Blake & The Eternals.
Something was missing.
I sang *gulls*, it sounded like *girls* in an English accent.
I sang *what is emptiness to what is no longer empty*.
We had no hits, obviously.
We were dropped in late spring
with the noise of a Coffee Mate clicking.
They'd *done the numbers*, and *No*.
It took a sleepless year in a stranger's basement
on Monticello not to kill myself.
I sang *I've done the numbers, and no*.
Our only song had been a poem about a man
holding a lantern at the end of a long hallway
lined with books and firewood.
He haunted me, as did his horse,
which all night would shift its legs,
stamping gently the floorboards. The song
was called "Farriers." I sang it
only once in Montana in late-August '89
as my father and I stood in a field
at dusk, and with the fog holding everything,
a yoke of starlight lifted from the horse,
weightless and lifetimes ago.

Jennifer Stewart Miller

# [We Can't] Save Everything

Yesterday on BBC radio,
I listened to the Namib desert—

grains of sand
tumbling down dunes at night.

\*

Another storm churns toward New Orleans—
at the house on the Mississippi where

we danced a marriage by a bonfire,
the swollen river drags on the house's stilts.

\*

Gorgeous words—

drought
deluge

\*

Someone has already imagined
a hopeful future in which

cellars expect to be cisterns
and houses learn to float.

\*

Frequency
Intensity

\*

# Jennifer Stewart Miller

July sun bakes my sister and me
as we walk in the park — my hair

heavy as drapes

\*

High humidity — my old dog
is panting and thirsty.

\*

As I ate breakfast, I read that in Chennai
the monsoon this year was weak —

aquifers sucked dry,
people sipping their air conditioners' drips.

\*

Satiation
Desiccation

\*

Dog-day cicadas,
the sounds they make.

\*

Some days I read the news
and my heart is Death-Valley dry —

other days,
it's been raining for weeks.

\*

Weather versus climate

\*

My son is moving to Miami.
As is the sea.

\*

A flood or a sinking ship—
the way water
starts to climb the stairs.

*

Old word: *antediluvian*
New word: *antidiluvian*

*

This winter, the town cut the beach's
parking lot back and built a dune.

Last night, a bluegrass band—
music spilling into the ocean.

A. Molotkov

# Complicit in Incompleteness

I'm moved by how  the world moves past me, grows  its new shapes, its  myriad threads. I long to disappear inside  myself – my door  so worn only the frame holds it in place.  The moment – and then,  its other side, its under-  pinnings before and after us. How  to imagine completely, without  being inside the imagined? An empty  bed. A narrow path  from heart to mouth to  a scolding blue sky. Broken  glass where skin might be. I'm moved  by how the world moves me. How  to love more completely  given another chance,  this one?

Alex Mouw

# Genesis 3

After crocodiles lumbered off the shaven toenails
of the Word, after the most manic thought
became all birds at once. After the oceans
were put to bed on simmer, and the sun

and stars sorted out their choreography.
After the after of time's trap door burst open
and covered the earth in wind—what?

A viral rot that spread like crazy?
You call it sin sometimes, which is,

without ever knowing what exactly,
knowing utterly that you are wrong
in a more fundamental way
than you can know.

After that, the blinds all snap upwards,
retreating to scrolls in their high, plastic cases.
Brightness enters the room as a raiding party.
This has answered no questions, so you wait

within a silence rich as the hollow
of an unbowed cello. It continues to snow,
which you think deserves to be part of any

abject falling into sin, but is only
a northern add-on. Plows are piling it up.

This is how it feels to be exiled: an acoustic guitar
played so softly you can hear

## Alex Mouw

the thumb pad dragged briefly across the string
as it releases a barely plucked note.
The scratch of metal and the middle C

between which almost no one would distinguish.
Yet one is music; the other, cold mechanics.
Where is this going? The chapter just ends

with a flaming sword spinning like a windmill.
It must have been gorgeous from far away.

Marcus Myers

## Our Love is a Delicate Material in a Cornell Box as Vast as the Sea
—*A Letter to My Daughter*

I will keep these missives and photos in a cloud.
An idea folded in to amuse you:
                        Our words and pictures

in no object we will ever touch.
                        Our ideas adrift
in an amorphous cache of our data.

We might wish our blood and air supply
were not already locked
                        in the closed systems
of our bodies just so
we might lodge our organs

in servers, forever.

Regarding *missive* and *cloud*: I will only use
these wispy nouns to watch the candela shift,
                        from serious to whimsy,

in your eyes. To see
the bluest sun
                in your pupils hammer the sea-

like body of what I imagine
as *gold leaf*, what I imagine the oceanic material
unconditional love is made of,
                        which I keep for you

## Marcus Myers

beneath my ribs, always, where we house
every beat in a Cornell box
with screaming lobsters wearing *Pinch the Cook* aprons,

where they dance and boil within those slow seconds
of my dad jokes, in which you roll your eyes,
                away from my ridiculous words
and toward the actual clouds.

Nawal Nader-French

# Mother as text

The textile is parchment and it is red: It is the skin of my mother's dress that I write on. It is the dissemination of all manner of textiles: texts that are an impossible calculation. That spread around until they attach and cover every inch of her skin. White with cherries glued into the filaments. A made-in-foreign country. A jute type material—something heavy that weighs you down and you cannot pick yourself up from it. It controls your movement. From the inside it is rough and it slowly leaves abrasions on the skin, and it has been stretched and pulled, beaten till translucent like the skin of a beloved animal.

Christopher Nelson

# To Certainty

How one inch beneath the surface the roots
make a kind of net, which I break
so that I can put you in, royal catchfly, so that
I might attend to your growing—given rain, given
light, luck, and, most difficult, my constancy—
so that I might look up from the dishes or
daydreaming and be a little stunned by
your shock of red, as on a stroll we come across
the aftereffects of a fistfight. And maybe,
with more summers, you'll be established,
and the hummingbirds will duel for your nectar
so that we can mistake it all for a dance—
a few more summers, which we should have.

Munir Niazi
translated from the Punjabi by Zafar Malik and Faisal Mohyuddin

# Today Too
*(Ajj Da Din Vee)*

Today too just passed by
No work done at all

From the east climbed the sun
The west the place it came to stand

Neither did I meet God's creation
Nor did I remember God

Neither did I pray my prayers
Nor did I sip a sip of wine

No joy, no gloom, no one came near,
I did not laugh, I did not cry

Today too
Just passed by

John A. Nieves

# Between Glaciers

*I want* you would yawn in your pajama-blanket (its little
feet cracking from growth and wear) *to walk between*

*the big ice*. You had seen it on TV, the high pass, the narrowed
        horizon. I, being older, wanted to tell you that your legs

            up there would beg your tiny body to lay down, how the blue-
            white ice would love you straight to death, would catch

you in the laziest game of freeze tag ever, Peter-Pan you
into the landscape like you lost stuffed animals

in the piles in your room. I never said *yeti* or *wendigo*. I never
        said *hypothermia* or *snow blindness*. Not that any of that would

            have helped. You toddled off, taller and taller, into concrete
            and currency, into mortgage and health insurance. And your legs

said lie down here, but there was too much turning, too much
heat and wind for anything to stay. And I never said *bankruptcy*

or *totaled car*. I never said *heartbreak* or *migraine*. Not that any
        of that would have done any good. Not that anything ever could.

Caleb Nolen

# Reunion

When I wake I'm in ninth grade again,
in the bare bleak hour before school.
It must be winter: outside my window
the fields fill with grey-blue light.
I dress slowly, tuck a pack of Marlboros
in my sock to smuggle past my mother,
and run the teeth of a handsaw across
my throat. I push and pull until my head
comes off. It happens so easily. No vertebrae
resist, no heart makes a messy spray. My head
doesn't weigh anything. I carry it to school
in the crook of my arm and walk straight
to our circle near the vending machines.
Everyone's there: Matt and Adam and Chris
and Dan. Even Mike and Bobby. Everyone
turns to look me over. Mike asks how
I managed not to die. I say I never will
as long as no one tears off my eyelids.
They all nod quietly and then Bobby
reaches for my face.

James Norcliffe

# The Museum of Unnatural History

can be seen through the mist at certain times of the day
on the danger side of the yellow line at the station platform.

Beyond the rails there are deserted streets where
deserted houses lean drunkenly against each other.

The last newspaper, driven by a gritty wind, flaps
down a road. The banner headline is obscured.

Ice falls from the trees like white petals and
the great, bare branches reach up struggling with

the memory of birds. The wind picks up, colder now,
lifting the paper. You'd almost think it was alive.

Eric Pankey

# The Entrepreneur

The day the war ends, he recalls each thin curl of maple that unfurled before the hand plane. He recalls the sawdust, tacky with humidity, as it fell from the ripsaw's blade. He recalls the shellac's soporific vapors. He awaits now the day the soldiers will return home in need of the crutches and prosthetic limbs he has crafted. At the start of the war, a mere carpenter, he had thought of specializing in coffin-making, but word of surprising advances in battlefield medicine made him think again.

M. Nasorri Pavone

# How to Motivate a Dog

A man owns show pigeons.
He talked about how once
when a prized bird got loose,
his dog chased and killed it.
To teach the dog, the man
tied the bird's body around
the animal's neck. He let it
hang there for a week.

*After that for the rest of its
life, the dog guarded my doves
better than God,* he said.
But he wasn't done. His son
at five chased a cherished
dove too. Where was the dog,
I didn't think to ask as
I'd already jumped ahead

to how, yes, the child hit it
with a stick until it was still.
How long the corpse hung
around the boy's neck he
didn't say, and his son, now
30, tells me how he hates
those birds but never why.
He watches over his father

better than God. And it wasn't
that his dad confessed
but affirmed: *humans are*

*animals*, not to suggest
an equation but to assert
which of the two is in charge
of both their training. He spends
a grand a month on bird food.

Marielle Prince

# In Order

In the ninth month of not bleeding, the cells of your spreadsheets flicker into chaos like a plain of crowded grasshoppers.

You wear sweaters to bed and wake up with a thermometer under your tongue, the slick of alcohol half dreamed into a stem of basil.

You remember being ten years old holding a warm washcloth between your legs while your kidneys throbbed an unseen siren.

You remember not knowing one thing from another, something fibrous on the toilet paper like a decades-old strand of saffron.

On the ultrasound you see that a room inside you has been filled to the walls with black balloons, waiting all this time to say surprise.

In the MRI your breath goes stale as if a cellar has been opened in the roof of your mouth, and a cloud of neon flaps its wings through your bloodstream.

Your grandmother prays on her own body and the spirit dissolves the gathered masses. You find a solid place and score the days against it.

The doctor inserts a thin tube into the middle of your tender alphabet and electrifies the x into a thundery purple midnight.

Driving home, the white line of the road strobes. Your friend hears the click of her egg releasing and your eyes are having so much fun at this party.

Charles Rafferty

# Asymmetry

The lopsided tree eventually topples, and the fiddler crab must carry its heavy, unmusical claw. Consider the pinched eyes of the flounder, how it must live and die without seeing the mud it rides. The world is full of ill proportions — a lack of balance, of fairness. If I tore away this bedroom roof, you'd see how the stars have mostly brightened the sky above your side.

Laura Ring

# Range of Absence

The Range of Absence sits in the southern corridor of the longest mountain belt in the world, spanning two continents. Also known as the "Eldrens," for these mountains are old. They have had time to divest themselves of surface. & what the elements reveal, the people mine. Tin. Silver. Gold.

You can't remove something and be surprised to leave a hole—a socket that once held a tooth, now a jammy absence that telegraphs pain. Dendritic husks. Walls of pulp falling in on themselves.

You can't see the damage from lower down, in the foothills or valleys—can't see the plateaus scraped hollow like a foundered womb; splayed veins camouflaged by soil and vegetation. Every inch of the Eldren slopes drips with green, because loss must sometimes hide beneath abundance.

The miners have gone, with their traded plumes. Hammered breastplates. Reed boats on ice-fed lakes. But there are those who stay. They are attuned to absence, the way it settles in their own scraped hollows, though they think themselves untapped.

It may not be possible to love something for the wrong reasons. Somewhere, even now, a condor raids a kill for the bones, leaves the meat.

Linwood Rumney

# *The Devens Literacy Test:* Do beds run?

Over the course of their long, unexceptional lives, they put on many faces, but never their own.

All gods depend on style.

We lurch toward them each day, instinctually flapping our poorly-fitted appendages, equally ill-suited for all habitats.

They half-rise to meet us, these otherwise unpopulated beaches revealed by the receding of light.

When we reach them, we clutch ourselves and lie down, and we lay— what else?—our *selves*, into hundreds of eggs.

They hatch as we sleep, for that is the meaning of sleep.

Most nights only one hatchling survives.

Our kind has flourished this way for millions of years.

Natasha Sajé

## slipskin
### — *Baltimore County*

on this narrow path along a river
a scent in crisp October

air hangs like a hood
unmistakable musk whips my head

toward its source   blotched yellow
wrinkled hairy leaves shield

bloomed dark purple grapes
wax rubs off with my thumb

someone lived here once grew fruit in land
razed of forest   allowed sun to sweeten it

even in shade the vine still bears
Concord after Ephraim Bull's northern town

to honor his crossing the vines
Leif Erickson saw on the coast of Vinland

north American *vitis labrusca* with *vinifera*
making a fox grape   the odor I ingest

more than three hundred years after natives
were pushed west while Africans

labored for the first Catholic Calverts
clearing woods and tilling land

growing fruit as big as wild plums
skin that slips off with my teeth

large seeds I swallow

Christopher Salerno

# Headfirst

Just a boy then, I was struck
    hard by a car and arced over

the roadside. Despite the pain I told
    no one. How the man driving

kept on driving. I hadn't yet found out
    about the body or velocity.

What a wound is, and how some bruises
    flower, spread like steam on the mirror

blurring all beauty. My mother
    says the '80s were terribly rapey.

She hisses into her rotary phone.
    Says a man may leave his voice

inside of a stranger forever, place something
    hard as a blood-flecked stone.

When I woke in the road, I rested
    my little chrome bicycle by the curb.

The smell of lilac, the sound of traffic
    starting up again in the street.

Shapes that keep us awake decades
    later. The fuck do I know about

all this thickness? Not the slant rhyme
    of fear & underwear. Haven't I

## Christopher Salerno

walked around with a killer's power,
        swaggering until now? But any boy's

teen years: days spent pursuant to puberty.
        The body as factory. I would

have driven high across this enormous
        darkness just to watch a woman

unbutton air. I should be writing this
        with fear, knowing I was danger.

Mara Adamitz Scrupe

## Nancy's Soliloquy/ Dr Lightfoot's Law of Dynamic Overlap/ Ivy Hill Plantation, 1853

I am a rare wind's howl over hummocks & others'
remains/ vestiges
      of the four last things
      of the dreariest of sins
debatable in the context of complicity
of semi-permanent
structures/ not buildings per se nor prescriptive

redemption       (*I am    a woman*)

     but hovels/ submission/ I'm   I'm
Nancy      servant      slave      woman's
body owned as I've never known it as you ever
do/ ever    a man

                     /

     I look at her
hard   (death judgement heaven   & hell) dread
     her devil but treat her
     nonetheless

in the season of her growing
rounder    I refer to parturition
euphemistically/ she made shift for herself      committing
this truss
                 /

# Mara Adamitz Scrupe

(capta      from *taken*     not    *given*)

/

think of the limbic allied to the biomechanical in dynamic
overlap     translate menials
into numbers/ rationed/ tined to the not-yet-discovered
     maladies to the jerk of a leg
     to the sweat of her limbs
     to covetousness & grievous/ copulation

birth      & ebb

/

(*I am*    *I am a woman*)

/

& in the end that's all but in between I diagnose
drapetomania in these creatures of laziness & sloth in these malarious
river regions/ same common as the stripe down an ass's back

/

(*I am a woman I am a woman Iam a woman Iam awomanIamawoman*)

/

     I refer too to contagion/ congenital in the nervous
system's disarray/ neurosyphlitic
indices to access quickly –

    & praxis/ my skills enacted        as her master
pays for quinine & blue mass for the ague &
the pox & ipecac for vomit
       & overlap cupping & venesection
       I see her six days straight it's nothing else but

                /

torrid tonight/ the air thick with the Chickahominy
River & China roses just budding
out & the sun falling down fast behind the mountains

                /

(& looking out & across      & so so
    light      I wonder to include *human*
     *& kindness*    oaths    I want to be convinced
I have faith/ trust I want to be delivered from      )

                /

behind this Blue Ridge    barricade
    bulky/ abundant    (I am I am    *I am*    )

---

NOTE: Blue mass was a 19th century concoction consisting of opium and mercury used as a treatment for common diseases like malaria and syphilis.

Drapetomania was a conjectural mental illness hypothesized by scientific racism as the cause of enslaved Africans fleeing captivity.

Mara Adamitz Scrupe

# thoughts on borders

                                            out beyond
the blest kingdom     following the trackless traders
& slavers & affluent technocrat's lands amassing     & bomb
shelters & clandestine

        airstrips & marble tomb bathrooms & vestigial
leftwing demonstrators & gated havens to get off

on         lizards dart in & out of cracks or lie benumbed amongst
burdock catch-spring/ stickled/ spurred
        ovate seeds/ burred bolls while reckless rule-less ghost moths

skim & lek/ scroll & whitecap/ billow & spray     exploding
in quiver-pleasured raves & gullies

            & out beyond

the blest kingdom insect/ amphibian/ mammalian females
        choose their mates     the males of the species
entice them/ uncontested none abstain     & in a homeland

convinced of its quiddities     mark & mind an ancient
détente as way off watching the eighty richest ride it out

it's a bad bad business     the walls say: *inhale exhale
expect nothing* smells that way     stink squirming in like
so much shit needing doing/ chill to the bone/ & the dam

diggers stem the flood     over the faceless fenced & the wounded
un-winged collapse & the orange peacock-eyed
butterflies restless remind me of rope & strand     of knot
    & sign & climb & hold on tight     for dear

*dear*   at the bottom of the breach/ holed & don't they
          know it & up here on top between damp squab & hassock

          common six-line racerunner skinks ricochet/ quick
queue form a line from my chaise across the resort porch/ not stiffs

          under a sand dune on the other side of a wall
but languidly marking a border        they simply     slip over

Maureen Seaton

## 4th Stage Metaphoric Breast Cancer

*Blah, blah, blah—metaphors.*
—Jack Nicholson, *The Bucket List*

Cancer is the dark era inside a diamond, the intrusive reign of a bully,
specific and preposterous, a river called Snake. It tastes like fruitcake.

Those who would destroy cancer cannot get past its beauty. Light
bows around it, that absolute desolate, that brilliant lack of conscience.

My doctor's name is Diamond, the opposite of cancer, though both
diamonds and cancer grow within a matrix: conflicting mythologies.

It takes the earth one to three billion years to grow a single diamond,
a metastable allotrope of carbon; while cancer grows out of nowhere,

a metastatic deconstructed trope of war, as in: *They lost their battle with.*
It's quite possible my doctor has never been in a poem before.

Or, if she has, it was more likely an epithalamium (for her wedding)
or an ode (to her genius), not a threnody (*wailing song*). They say there's

logic behind the existence of cancer, but I try not to think about it,
especially as it relates to metaphor, therefore poetry, therefore me.

If I could talk to cancer as it tokes its smoky residue up my spine,
hijacking life, I'd say: Here's your bus pass, here's the key to my car.

I predict I'll be sliced from head to hip one day to find a big open field
with Ferris wheel, carousel, and Steeplechase: Coney Cancer Island.

I am its host and dearest friend. And it is powerfully quiet inside me.
Time bomb, pied-à-terre, heart speaking soundlessly to its beloved.

Tsuji Setsuko
translated from the Japanese by Taylor Mignon and Andrew Houwen

# Metallic Logic

like a Chinese emperor
using a folded fan
to handle a slanted reticence

while staring at the back of a fish
the vertical assembling of a rainbow

as for the sadness within the silence
the sea's horizon cuts the sky like a razor

Donna Spruijt-Metz

# I need the long march

When I was my grandmother's mother I knew
she would be beautiful in the time of war
so I set to knitting her

a whole skein of swans
in flawless V formation

pearl-colored
to match her skin,
steadfast guides for the long march

I sewed coins and jewelry into the hem of her dress
copal, charms, carnelian and ash
into her long sleeves

and when my fear for her life was bigger
than my love
I released her to the steppes and flew

above it all, above the war, grasslands
snowfields, past the small horses
and the gray wolves

Seth Stephanz

# Secular Liberal Democracy

A horse, a carriage, which goes first?
To know for sure, we must
consult the instruction booklet.
Their hooves are clobbering the cobblestones,
just like a bully clobbers a nerd or a whisk
clobbers yolk—but hey, you can't make a cake
with clobbered shale but you can make more
road with it, but here's the thing:
it might not be so easily clobberable.

Another cool thing
that you might not have considered:
a cake can be served at a wedding.
This is voluntary, of course, something
one may opt in or out of as is a necessary
feature within a secular liberal democracy.
Propagandists have attempted to slander this model
with a "layer-cake" of sorts, wherein
there are the rich that "eat for you,"
the soldiers who "shoot you," etc.,
with the working people pulling
the "charabanc of the well-to-do," or whatever.

Well, you can't make a cake with the bourgeoisie,
if there is anything that Marx has taught me—but hey,
I went to culinary school. Like the purging flame
of justice, like the open palm of equality, one goes
before the other, is my intuition, just like you
have got to add some ingredients
before others if you want things to end up right.

### Seth Stephanz

Like for instance, if baking a bombe
Alaska, you have to add sponge cake before the rum,
otherwise it just doesn't turn out
right, like a road made out of dough, or
something. It's just not something horsable,
or clobberable, or exploitable—you know,
roads are for something, after all.

Lisa Gluskin Stonestreet

# Ripe

as in the fruit bowl, the flies, a child asking
*but it can be unripe again*

*right?*

O sweet boy how to tell you what the world
will tell you anyway and soon

each hand of the clock, its slow swoop
up toward midnight,

dusk and what follows. The soft spot
at the stem of the peach.

Marcela Sulak

# Genesis

Running along the beach Tuesday, I see the arc of the kingfisher
wagging against the sky like the gray eyebrow of God.

He is looking for his fish.
And God is simply looking.

Suddenly he points and drops,
stabs the surface of the sea and disappears.

And in the grass a hoopoe plunges its bill,
pulling it open, and the small earth splits.

I love the kingfisher's undulating flight,
the wings half close at the end of each beat.

I love how it beats with my feet.
And God stands by, still waiting for news.


\*


Friday Joseph and I are naming our beasts. Joseph says before
the transit camps his family had been used to owning things,

and also that he'd been pretty for a long time—that's why he'd not
burnt out as bad as the others. Joseph says he resents it now that he's not.

Pretty was hard to lose. I think he's still pretty, but I know
what he means—now we are promised, no longer "promising."

He says that when his book is done, he may not have another in him.
God says he may not have another book in Godself either.

\*\*

I am sitting on the balcony with my tanned, bare legs up,
ankles crossed. It's Friday night, I am resting,

like God. And so are my thighs,
which God made, and which I sculpted. They're not bad

at this angle in the dark, resting from their daily run,
and resting from having given birth,

and from wearing high heels to climb the crumbling cemetery walls
throughout the capital cities of Europe.

They are resting from carrying home the enormous pink yam
I grew last year in my garden, and which my neighbors implied

I did not deserve to grow. And resting from carrying around all the women
I am not, this one, for example, whose legs are longer than mine

and slim in their musculature and sexy as hell next to the legs of someone I love
in this photo from last month. But then I remember the ones

I love are usually more exciting in my imagination than they are in real life,
and I decide to let it go. See, this is what I mean, God, by rest.

And this morning, running alongside the river full
of Egyptian ducks and gulls, the air heavy with moisture,

I came upon a beautiful man riding a bike, carrying
a bouquet of wild flowers. As he passed me he called out low,

## Marcela Sulak

"Kol ha-kavod." Usually people only tell you you're doing a good job
when you obviously are not, and maybe you look like the effort

will kill you. But what does he know,
I'm doing a damn fine job now. I'm resting.

It's just the sort of thing God would say.

Paige Sullivan

# Ascension with Box of Chocolates

Over my right shoulder I glimpse the couple
sharing a box of sweets as the plane
hurtles down the runway, obliquely noses up,
fuels itself into the sky, the conifers below
receding to small, dark triangles, then
pinpricks. My husband is across the aisle
from me, surfing movies, and I'm playing
the same lonely song on repeat, not because
I'm sad, but because something about it
untethers me, lets me submerge myself in
the hot bath of a mood, memories of past
moments in the dark. Like when someone
else's memory of you becomes your memory
of yourself. As in, that night I pulled up
in my Oldsmobile, sat in blue shorts
on the closed trunk. Maybe my tires
had kicked up dirt that was settling
as you walked out the front door, toward me.
How a body can hold all that want,
let it mutate and dissipate. It's mostly
shame now, years of not speaking, with more
to come. This year, a decade since we met.
Planes are mostly fine, with occasional lapses
into terror if I think too much about
this soup can barrel of metal in the sky,
serene flight attendants our shepherds
in plum designer uniforms. *Too smart
for my own good*, a dentist once told me
when the anesthetic shots weren't enough—
that perhaps the mind works around the work-
arounds to discern the pain that must surely be
there. Felt. It's different than pressing your
thumb into a healing bruise, I promise.

Elizabeth Sylvia

# Coumadin

Repeating every morning the liturgy
Name on the bottle, a science of the heart.
On every bottle the liturgy of science,
The repeating heart names the morning.
The pink milk out of the glass dropper
Runs behind the pearl-teeth to the heart.
Milk of the glasspink heart, behind the teeth
A pearl runs out to the dropper.
The medicine has become a touch of God,
The drug-veined body, a lockbox for the cracked heart.
God cracked the body, veined the heart. Touch the box
Of drug, for the medicine has become the lock.
Heart. Heart. Heart. Repeating becomes the medicine,
A dropper of morning. Names run out of the teeth.
Milk touches the pink body, pearl of the drug.
On every bottle, science has a lock
For the veined box, a cracked
Liturgy to the God inside the glass.

Andrew Szilvasy

# Snow Day, with Oranges

I learn about the energy market to win an internet argument with a user named FartMan69.

I lose.

I play *Risk* online with friends. One makes the *Princess Bride* joke and I don't laugh because in this game they're all land wars.

I lose.

I print scholarly articles that I won't read.

I watch the last three minutes of a UConn game on Youtube. They lose.

I sit and try to sketch the trees in my backyard, but instead I imagine the Arch of Constantine. In front is a ring of fire out of which a white tiger leaps at Mickey Mouse.

I am riding that tiger, though I look different astride him: big muscles and flowing hair like He-Man, and I carry the Power Sword in one hand and a copy of Keats's poems in the other.

I make lunch.

I eat oranges.

I become obsessed with finding beautiful pictures of the dead.

I fall in love first with Maude Fealy, then Helene Anna Held, then an unnamed creole woman posed like a fayum mummy portrait and then I fall in love with one of the mummy portraits backed by gold.

I imagine I've stolen the DeLorean to go back to meet her. Her name is Berenice and I think of Callimachus. I could use this device to visit him and bring back some lost work; part of me thinks I'd make money like Biff, but no one cares about Callimachus anymore and without gas the DeLorean is as useless as a rotten orange.

# Andrew Szilvasy

I bet on who the next emperor will be and win big.

I avoid Pompeii.

I make up stories about the future. There are flying cars I tell her.

I explain a car.

I participate in the lioness and the cheese grater.

I watch our children play among reeds and I tell them that Cleopatra is closer to us in time than she is to the Pyramids. They are unimpressed.

I make a Prince Albert in a can joke. Nobody laughs.

I feel at home for the first time in years.

I age and watch my children become merchants. It is wonderful to watch them fall in love. One daughter-in-law worked in a pub. Their beer is bad: sour, yeasty, and flat.

I drink it.

I'm convinced that I am my own ancestor.

Shuzo Takiguchi
translated from the Japanese by Mary Jo Bang and Yuki Tanaka

# LINES

red-plated fish skillfully collide head-on in the intersection,

that's when you hide your face

in a fine-tuned gasping

a rose becomes weighty and downcast

and the tigress splits

[…]

the reed makes a deal

with the clarinet's ordeal

changing the inclination

of evening showers that know what's up with a pearl shell

[…]

on the morning streets a dented girl moves side to side

exciting purple glasses

setting fire to some rosette petals

memories of longing for the Botticelli boy

pressing in on her gilt-floral chaplet

her beauty mark mole is so blue it makes up the mind of the wind

Shuzo Takiguchi
translated from the Japanese by Mary Jo Bang and Yuki Tanaka

# basse élégie
# [low-down elegy]

If one salutes the fragile flower petals of the sweet-pea as one turns at sea, a really fun-filled funeral procession will face the *eau-de-cologne* sun and twist around. A wing digs in like an endless *éternité*. Say thanks to the unruffled winter-white lily. The snowdrop crystal on the front, capable of drifting away like a consecrated wafer, flits back-&-forth like a jitterbugging belle. If only a starry ray of played-out music is stabbing thy pale-bone ankles. Seen creeping in the frosted-pane window, that has already nodded off in order to reply, some farm hand passes through unnoticed. O, snow-white-farmer dost thou love sweet-peas? His smile digs in like a wing. His beauty-mark mole, unable to distinguish a pearl earring from a flight of steep steps, finally lies down and dies at the last feast. Let that Alexander who's already moved to the rear of the spectrum fully understand the mole buried deep beneath the thick-as-thieves cover of dew.

Eric Tran

# Hippocampus

       From Greek,

sea monster

       (*sic* see monster)

In my mother's

       tongue *I remember*

trans. *I miss*

       My tongue pared

lemon rind

       scorched

in sugar

       First peat

then trenchant

       then copper

then plosive

       then whimper

then

       then

then

Leah Umansky

# Tyrant as Self Reflection

The tyrant sees himself when *he* sees you. He sees himself when he sees *you*. He *sees* himself when he sees *you*. Himself. *You*. Himself. *You*. Himself. *You*. Himself. *You*. Himself. *You*. Himself. The tyrant lives in the tyranny of *you*. The tyrant lives in the country of *you*. The tyrant lives in the you, in you. The you that the tyrant brings out, is the tyrant's *version* of you. The tyrant lives in the *you* he sees in himself. In the you he *sees*. In the you *he* sees. In the *you* he sees in you. In the you that is *not* you. In the you that is *him*. His outrage lies in *your* control. When the tyrant sees your control, he sees the control *he* desires. When the tyrant sees *your* love, he sees the love *he* desires. When the tyrant sees *your* love, he sees *his* love. When the tyrant sees *your* love, he *doesn't* see love, he doesn't *see* love, he *sees* himself. He sees the love he desires *for* himself. He sees the love he desires for *himself*. He sees the love he desires to feel. He sees his *own* love. He sees his self-love; he sees his reflection in *your* love. When the tyrant splits, he doesn't split for you, he splits to *better* himself. He splits into two, for two of him is better than one. He splits into two to see two reflections of *his* beautiful self. He sees himself butterflied. He sees the mirror of his beauty duplicated. The mirror of his beauty *is* the mirror of his lies. The mirror of his truth and his want. He *sees* the mirror and the way *out* of the mirror. He sees the mirror and he sees *you*, but the *you* he sees is himself. He sees himself, his self, his self *and* his self-reflection. His authority, his charisma, his availability and his cooing are all ways he attracts himself to himself, like a moth to a flame. In his attraction is *his* attraction to you. In his attraction is his *attraction* to you. He is attracted to you because he sees his own self-reflection in *your* truth, in *your* confidence, in *your* talent. When the tyrant says he *is* going to hurt you, he *is going to* hurt you, *he* is going to hurt you, he is going to hurt you, but he is *also* going to hurt himself. When the tyrant hurts you, he hurts himself. When he hurts *you*, he hurts himself, but in *your* hurt, he only sees his *own* hurt and, in *his* hurt, he sees himself and *not* you. When the Tyrant sees *you*, he sees himself. He *sees* you, but *mostly* sees himself. He sees himself. He sees himself *in* you. He sees *him* in you. He sees and sees and sees, but *only* sees himself. He sees your hands on him and he sees *his* hands on you. In his hands, he sees his hands, but he doesn't see them holding you. He sees *himself* in his hands. He sees himself holding himself. And when you cry, the tyrant hears his *own* cry. He wants to match your cry with *his* cry because in *your* cry is the tyrant's cry. In *your* cry, is the *more* beautiful cry and that is the cry of the tyrant, his reflection. In your cry, is the reflection of himself. In your cry, in your release, in your orgasm is the letting-go that *he* desires. *Your* letting go, makes him lose control. He sees *his* letting go in yours, but he also sees the control *you* lack and in *your* lack is *his* lack and in *your* lack, he sees *his* lack and in *your* lack, he sees himself. *In you, he sees himself.* In your admiration, is his admiration. In your admiration, is his own admiration of *himself.* In your rise, is the tyrant's rise. In your fall, is the tyrant's fall. In your buckling is his buckling. In your wetness is the wetness he wishes *he* had. In your secrets, are his secrets. In your willing, is *his* willing. In your tease, is his tease. In you, the tyrant sees himself. He sees his platform, his hope, his fear, his solidarity and his piousness. In *you*, he sees himself atomized. In you, he sees his fears denounced. In *your* happiness, he sees *his* happiness, and the happiness he *could* have if he didn't see *his* lack. In *your* victories, his own victories. In *your* goodness, his *own* goodness, and his *own* goodness in you. He sees his *own* creativity, his *own* mechanisms turning, and his own mechanisms turning *in* you. In you, he sees his own buttress of rules landsliding. In his landslide, he sees *your* lack and in *your* lack is *his* lack. In affecting you, he is affecting himself. In accommodating you, he is accommodating himself. In working on himself, he is *only* working on himself, he is only working *on* himself, he is only working on *his self*. His *self*. In working on himself, he is manipulating himself, he is mastering himself to his self; he is mounting himself, look, he is mouthing something to his self: *I am you; I am the tyrant.*

Alia Hussain Vancrown

# Funeral Home

My brother wants it to be a family business,
so I work part-time on weekends. My job
is to stand at the foot of the casket and
offer tissues to the viewers. My mother
stands at the head. I'm too sensitive.
I can't connect with sleeping faces. Sometimes
mourners faint and I catch them. I use
sage throughout the room so the spirits
don't touch my skin. My brother embalms
the bodies. Sometimes a hand will jerk up
from pressure of the fluid, a final wave to this side.
My brother talks to them like living people
as he fixes their hair, makeup, clothes.
Sometimes gases leave them, and it sounds
like agonal breathing. My brother wears gloves
and a smock so the diseases don't touch his skin.
I'm just doing this part-time. I do all my crying
before the families get there. So far the sage has worked.
If there's any freakish thing whatsoever, I'm not
going into the family business full-time.

Hannah VanderHart

# My Mother's Brown Plaid Drapes

Hung midway
in the house

of my one life,
dividing

time from
space:

before my
brother

touched
my sister

and then my
other sister

it is always
autumn

in that house,
the light

walnut,
hickory

listen: a leaf
falls there

and I want
to push

# Hannah VanderHart

pause
on the cassette

player,
hear

the machine
click

into its
soft hum

the curtains
still        hung

Anastasia Vassos

## the modern poet tries to read Sappho in ancient greek

] yes

] on a soft bed

] one
     cycladic beckon [     ] found

] not found


     ] yearns
          her virginity

*O for Adonis*

] lyre
          ] necessary limb [

] *bride with beautiful feet*


] pearls
     unstrung

] Orpheus ungrounded [     ] decoded


] imaginal [     ] smears
          hands dip [     ] yes

Anastasia Vassos

] language
        ] lingual
                ] languor
                        ] linger

] lost [       ] soft

] ah ah Sappho

*stand to face me beloved and open out [*

*the grace of your eyes*

and so [       ] sensate dream

        ] and these fingertips

and on these eyes [   ] yes

        *black sleep of night*

words linger now [   ] yes
                ] tongue lips bloom on ear

*may you sleep on the breast of your delicate friend*

Mark Wagenaar

# It Was While I Was Looking at the Oldest Wooden Wheel Ever Discovered

I got a phone call from a detective
who said my husband had been busted
with a thousand painkillers, my fare said
as we pulled away from the airport,
what's changed in five thousand years?
I had pegged her for a tourist, thought she'd ask
about Sniper Alley, as they all do, & instead
I had nothing to say. No one ever says how much
we miss the war, I said, & regretted it.
But it's true. I don't know when the statues
will weep again. Or when we'll see flowers
handpainted on a yellow-lettered *Pazi Snajper!* sign.
Once, she replied, I was in a boat on the Iška
& drifted by the ruins of prehistoric
pile-dwellings—stumped stilts in the water.
It was like this, she waved at the cars, looking up
at everyone as they faded away.
There was an orchard that survived the shelling—
once, in spring, it was all in wedding white
I replied but she had already climbed out.
And the map my mother kept—
who said *I always knew I was Croatian*,
who said with a grin *the Polish took all our vowels*,
the map was pigeon bones hanging
from ceiling-tied strings, like wind chimes.
Red strings knotted to some of the bones,
each knot someone who vanished.
Weeks, months, it was like looking down the throat

Mark Wagenaar

of a dovecote for cardinals. Like a snapshot
of the whirlwind of souls if each shade
were robed in red. Then an outline emerged:
What looked like a feather. Then two feathers,
three, more, then the long red strands
of my mother's hair. I stood before it
& tried to remember what bread was like.
A map of my mother. My country. Everyone
we had lost. I remember it shook with the wind
that blew in from the missing windows.
Whistle of incoming, clinking rain of shingles
& concrete. I remember she tied a red string
around my wrist. I remember whispering *remember me*
out the window, into tomorrow's one good ear.

Claire Wahmanholm

# Metamorphosis with Milk and Sugar

Every day I pump 84 ounces of milk from my body.
Every day I am filled with, and empty myself of,
the liquid equivalent of a small baby. My eyes sting
as the milk leaves my body. That is the prolactin,
sweetening everything my brain touches. That book
is sweet, those peonies on the table are sweet, the baby
is so sweet that my eyes leak when they brush against her.

I have spent so much time putting so much milk
into the baby that I don't remember when water started
to taste bitter. Like drinking from a hot, reedy pond.
More and more I find myself standing before
the open refrigerator. The milk is 38 degrees and sweet
as ice cream. The faucet rusts over. I cover it
with a dishcloth. I only have eyes for milk.

My brain finds this craving a little too neat,
but that doesn't matter. I am almost always in
the dairy aisle. I am almost always in the parking lot,
lifting the jug to my mouth with both hands.
It blocks out the sun like a sweet cold moon.
I can hear my throat squeezing in my ears as I swallow
and swallow. I imagine myself filling with milk
from the feet up: my ankles cool to the touch,
my knees sweetening, my stomach a marble sea.
When I look at myself in a windshield I see it is real,
I see my face is pearly and trembling.

### Claire Wahmanholm

Though I am made of milk, I can still walk
to the store. I walk very slowly, as if at the bottom
of a swimming pool. I walk slowly so I do not spill.
I am so cold that my eyes fog up when I step outside.
My skin beads like a cold bottle. I am slick in my shoes.

Whenever I see the baby, my eyes frost over
like snow cones. They leave a dusting of sugar on
everything they touch. In my new sugar house, I pick
rock candy grit from the corners of the baby's eyes,
wipe syrup from her nose, brush brown sugar from
her velvet hair. Each night I flick more and more ants
from behind her ears. Each morning more and more
of the baby has disappeared.

Jessica L. Walsh

# Blood Gutter

If Bubba has a real name it's Bubba.
When my knife year comes I speak it three times—
he's the guy, with signs at church and Bonser's.
My mother responds [*quiet*] then [*sigh*]
then *Jesus. Not Bubba. No fucking way.*
*I took the kitchen knives there once, but you*
*couldn't see wall for confederate flags.*
She pauses and says, *And other shit.*
*Other shit* is swastikas or klan flags.
She doesn't want me to be from a place
like the place I'm from. She curtains the words.
When my dad comes in, it's all *neverminds*.
*Take mine—I can't imagine you'd need it.*
We all imagine. We don't say the words.

Mike White

## Load-Bearing

Measuring the house,
her half, my half,
timber by timber,

a green inchworm.

# John Sibley Williams

# Carcinogen

Lately, an infertile valley. An old war-
damaged church. Naught, as in

the lungs can't hold it all in
anymore. Breath, as in a fawn

scraping her dry tongue raw
on red arroyo sands. The bullet

another's hunger pushes deep
into her hide. A mother

who tries to inhale the world
away, porchside, pluming

like the smoke stacks dad
says define (as in not

disrupt, beautify
maybe) this

afterthought of horizon.
To fail,

is what I mean,
at owning one's face.

As in *tell me everything
you need to ruin to make*

# John Sibley Williams

*a body livable again.* To live in it,
lately, after its ruin (steeple

snapped off, this hollowed
fist of land unclenching,

deer skin stretched over
the mantle, all one's violences

contained in a single cell, finally,
spreading). As in the birds

draw their arrows back. Fire. *Fire.*
The air, I mean. That sting.

Caitlin Wilson

# Geyser

*Disillusioned* is my favorite word,
a mirror's vocation. Mine is round

as a pore, silver as my kitchen shears.
A landscape of elemental cold.

This dog is white as the frozen bends
of Paint Branch stream—where ice

is a connective tissue I rarely
see in Maryland, despite

January. She doesn't love me.
We walk on rock salt and asphalt.

A dog can't recognize
herself in a mirror,

won't touch her own face, examine
her tail. Speculate on length and width.

Again, and again they ask me
*what is she?—what is she called?*

I feed her the oval of a hardboiled egg
and pretend her name is Kentucky;

the consonants like kissing. Younger,
I kissed no one, was exhaust smoke

### Caitlin Wilson

haunting sunlight after the car departs. Mirrors
too lightless to reflect this

when my mother
covered the windows,

said a red sunrise was lovely, how she hoped
her head would *geyser across the living room.*

Kentucky's quartz teeth gentle on my palm,
even in her greed. But could I love her.

Shannon K. Winston

# Notes from the Pantry, 1990

1.

There was Clorox and darkness.

2.

Strawberry and blueberry preserves in mason jars, too. One stacked on top of the other.

3.

Crackers and marbles. A deck of cards.

4.

It was like being in a Joseph Cornell box. My favorite, his *Untitled (Pharmacy) 1943*: a cabinet of medicine jars arranged 5 down, 4 across.

5.

Separate containers for a pink candy wrapper, a yellow butterfly wing, a seashell, a small painted city on curled paper.

6.

Maybe there was also a feather and coral. I'm not sure.

7.

Or perhaps it was olives and cranberries.

8.

Tenses, too, must be stored separately.

9.

Always, this scene returns on repeat: me, in the pantry, searching for the vacuum. My father appears suddenly in the doorframe.

10.

An egg, a branch, newspaper clippings.

11.

As if whispering into a confessional, he says: I have another wife and soon a son.

12.

Don't tell your mother.

13.

Water chestnuts, purple ribbon, flower seeds.

14.

My sticky hands let go of the vacuum.

15.

Just ten, I wondered: could I bottle this secret?

16.

Leave it here, in this box of boxes.

17.

Hula-hoops, tweezers, fake pearls.

18.

My father slips salt and a miniature scale into my palm.

19.

Close your eyes. Hold these parting gifts fast:

20.

Anger, a Tarot card, despair, two painted quail eggs.

Jane Zwart

# Grief is the gouge

From the runnel I know
for the route that grief runs

I have swept the salt. I have
stacked at the sluice's edges

the relics matured
into *memento mori*:

the feather in a heavy box,
an incidentaloma.

Not that the coulter could not
unstop the trench itself

but since the mortal is a rattle
that won't stop shaking

why not tidy, as if that were the same
as readiness? The rapids

you shoot to enter the world
and the rapids you shoot

to leave it—what slow going
they can be, after all.

And then there is the chute
you take to stay in the world.

I am sitting at the top of it now
knowing (but not knowing how)

the course will scrape me again
and I it, fearing drowning

and worrying what the torrent
will quench. Grief is the gouge

we carry downstream.

Martha Zweig

# Version of Charlotte

Slowpoke river delivered a broken corsage
to the frogs. Grunts garbled
one to the next like whispers-
down-the-lane: *panic* to *picnic*.

Everybody could see that flamboyant
sunset slumped in the mud. *No evening
around here steps out dressed like that. You ought
to be ashamed.* You'd better hope
I don't tell. But I'll tell.

She sprang into the spotlights, except
that her endless unraveling
hair tangled up in the trapeze. By then
she was the only mother
I had left and I left her behind.

# CONTRIBUTORS' NOTES

**DOHA ABOUL-FOTOUH** is a poet and pediatrician in training. She graduated from Rice University magna cum laude with a BA in English Literature, and won the American Academy of Poets First Prize for her poetry. Her passion within medicine is working with children with medical complexity and special needs.

**JOSE A. ALCANTARA** has worked as a bookseller, mailman, commercial fisherman, baker, carpenter, studio photographer, door-to-door salesman, and math teacher. His poems have appeared in *Poetry Daily, The Southern Review, Rattle,* and the anthologies 99 *Poems for the* 99% and *America, We Call Your Name: Poems of Resistance and Resilience.*

**LI BAI** (701-762 AD) was one of the most prominent Chinese language poets of the Tang Dynasty. Almost a thousand poems, including many written during his travels along the famed Silk Road, are attributed to him.

**MARY JO BANG** is the author of eight books of poems—including A *Doll for Throwing, Louise in Love,* and *Elegy,* which received the National Book Critics Circle Award—and a translation of Dante's *Inferno,* illustrated by Henrik Drescher. She teaches creative writing at Washington University in St. Louis.

**MICHELE BARON**, world-traveler, Fulbright Scholar, author, visual/performance artist, is again relocating after having lived three years along the Silk Road in Central Asia, and another year journeying the roads between. Itinerant seeker of knowledge, developer of outreach projects, she prefers sensible shoes to heels.

**CAROLINE PARKMAN BARR** is a North Alabama native and a graduate of the MFA Writing Program at the University of North Carolina at Greensboro, where she served as Poetry Editor of *The Greensboro Review.* Her poetry has appeared or is forthcoming in *North Dakota Quarterly, Harbor Review, Sinking City,* and *Two Hawks Quarterly.* She is the Social Media Specialist for *Poetry Northwest* and lives in Oakland, California.

**HEATHER BARTLETT** is a professor of English and Creative Writing at the State University of New York College at Cortland. Her recent work has appeared in *Carolina Quarterly, Lambda Literary, Los Angeles Review, Redivider, Ninth Letter,* and other journals. She lives, writes, and grades papers in Ithaca, New York.

**MATSUO BASHŌ** (1644-1694), is known as the greatest master of Japanese haiku, the most famous poet of the Edo period.

**ASHWINI BHASI** is from Kerala, India. Her poems have appeared in journals such as *Room, Rogue Agent, Driftwood,* and *The Feminist Wire.* She is the winner of *Dunes Review*'s William J. Shaw Memorial Poetry Prize and the 2018 Voices of Color Poetry Fellowship from Martha's Vineyard Institute of Creative Writing.

**BONNIE BILLET** wrote until her late thirties, during which time she was published in *Poetry, Pequod,* and the *Kansas Quarterly.* Upon retirement, she has started writing again, and has been published in *So to Speak* and *Yes Poetry.*

**JESSE BREITE**'s poetry has appeared in *Crab Orchard Review, Terrain,* and *Prairie Schooner.* His chapbook is *The Knife Collector,* and he is an associate editor for *The Good Works Review.* He is also librettist for Atlanta composer Michael Kurth's scores. Jesse lives and teaches in Atlanta.

**CASSANDRA J. BRUNER**, the 2019-2020 Jay C. and Ruth Halls Poetry Fellow, earned an MFA from Eastern Washington University. A transfeminine poet and essayist, their writing appeared in, or is forthcoming from, *Black Warrior Review, Crazyhorse, Muzzle, Ninth Letter,* and elsewhere. Their chapbook, *The Wishbone Dress,* is available through Bull City Press.

**BEVERLY BURCH**'s third poetry collection, *Latter Days of Eve,* won the John Ciardi Poetry Prize and was published in 2019. Her first, *Sweet to Burn,* won a Lambda Literary Award and the Gival Poetry Prize. Her second, *How a Mirage Works,* was a finalist for the Audre Lorde Award. Poetry and fiction appear in *Denver Quarterly, New England Review, Willow Springs, Salamander, Tinderbox, Mudlark,* and *Poetry Northwest.*

**CATHERINE CARTER**'s most recent collection is *Larvae of the Nearest Stars* (LSU Press, 2019). Her work has also appeared in *Best American Poetry 2009, Ecotone, Orion, Poetry,* and *Ploughshares,* among others. She is a professor of English at Western Carolina University.

**KATHLEEN CASEY** is a visual artist and emerging poet living nervously in the shadow of several dozing volcanoes in the Pacific Northwest.

**LUISA CAYCEDO-KIMURA** is a Colombian-born writer, translator, and educator. She was a John K. Walsh Residency Fellow at the Anderson Center, an Adrienne Reiner Hochstadt Fellow at Ragdale, and a Robert Pinsky Global Fellow. Her poems appear in *The Cincinnati Review, Sunken Garden Poetry 1992-2011, Mid-American Review,* and elsewhere.

**AVRAHAM CHALFI** (1904-1980) was born in Lodz, Poland. He arrived in Israel in 1924 and worked in agriculture and road construction. He joined the worker's theater, Ohel, when it opened in 1925, and in 1953 became a member of the Tel Aviv Cameri municipal theater. He began publishing poems in 1933. Many of his poems were set to music by Arik Einstein and became evergreen popular songs of the Israeli charts.

**SUSANNA CHILDRESS** is the author of *Jagged with Love*, awarded the Brittingham Prize, and *Entering the House of Awe*, from New Issues, and a forthcoming book of essays with Awst Press titled *Extremely Yours*. Find her work at *The Rumpus, Iron Horse, Image, Best American Poetry, Relief,* and *Oakland Review*.

**ANTHONY DiCARLO** is a fourth year undergraduate at the University of California at Davis, currently pursuing a degree in Classical Languages and Literature. He has had work previously published in *Blue Marble Review* and was the 2019 winner of the Celeste Turner Wright Poetry Prize.

**RUTH DICKEY**'s first book, *Mud Blooms*, was selected for the MURA Award from Harbor Mountain Press. The recipient of a Mayor's Arts Award from Washington, DC, and a grant from the DC Commission on the Arts and Humanities, Ruth lives in Seattle and is Executive Director of Seattle Arts & Lectures.

**LISA DORDAL** is the author of *Mosaic of the Dark*, which was a finalist for the 2019 Audre Lorde Award for Lesbian Poetry. Her poetry has appeared in *Best New Poets, Ninth Letter, CALYX, The Greensboro Review,* and *Vinyl Poetry*. She teaches at Vanderbilt University. Her website is lisadordal.com.

**WENDY DREXLER**'s third poetry collection, *Before There Was Before*, was published by Iris Press in 2017. Her poems have appeared or are forthcoming in *The Atlanta Review, Barrow Street, J Journal, Nimrod, Prairie Schooner, Salamander, The Mid-American Review, The Hudson Review, The Threepenny Review, The Worcester Review,* and *Valparaiso Poetry Review*, among others; featured on *Verse Daily* and WBUR's *Cognoscenti*; and included in numerous anthologies. She's the poet in residence at New Mission High School in Hyde Park, Massachusetts.

**DYLAN ECKER** is working on an MFA at Miami University of Ohio. In 2019, he won the Jordan-Goodman Prize for poetry. His poems have been published in *Hobart, The Penn Review,* and elsewhere. He has a small collection of rocks situated above the kitchen sink.

**KELLY EGAN**'s poems have appeared in *Colorado Review, Laurel Review, White Stag,* and *Denver Quarterly*, and her manuscript was recently a finalist in the Midwest Chapbook Contest. She lives in San Francisco and has an MFA in Poetry from Saint Mary's College in Moraga. She likes to think about outer space and visit small towns.

**BRYCE EMLEY** is the author of the prose chapbooks *A Brief Family History of Drowning* (winner of the 2018 Sonder Press Chapbook Prize) and *Smoke and Glass* (Folded Word, 2018). He works in marketing at the University of New Mexico Press and is Poetry Editor of *Raleigh Review*. Read more at bryceemley.com.

**KRISTINA FAUST** is a native New Jerseyan living in Grand Rapids, Michigan. Her poems have appeared recently in *The Common, Blackbird, Harvard Review, Mid-American Review, Washington Square Review,* and elsewhere. She received the 2018 Disquiet Literary Prize for poetry.

**ANDREW FITZSIMONS** has published two volumes of poetry, *What the Sky Arranges* (Isobar Press, 2013), and *A Fire in the Head* (Isobar Press, 2014). *The Sunken Keep*, his version of Giuseppe Ungaretti's *Il Porto Sepolto*, was published by Isobar Press in 2017. *The Complete Haiku of Bashō* is forthcoming from Isobar.

**MAJDA GAMA** is a Saudi-American poet based in the Washington, DC area. Her poetry has appeared in *Beloit Poetry Journal, The Fairy Tale Review, Hunger Mountain, Nimrod, The Normal School,* and *Slice.* She is a "Best of the Net" nominee and a poetry editor at *Tinderbox*.

**HENRY GOLDKAMP** is from St. Louis. Recent work appears in *Indiana Review, Diagram,* and *Notre Dame Review.* He is recipient of the 2019 Academy of American Poets Award and the Ryan Chighizola Prize from the University of New Orleans. His public art projects have been covered by *Time* and NPR.

**MARIAM GOMAA** is a physician and the author of *Between the Shadow & the Soul* (Backbone Press). Her writing has appeared in *Time*, NBC News, *Doximity, Nimrod, Graze Magazine, Readings for Diversity and Social Justice 4e,* and more. Her work is an exploration of womanhood, intersectional identity, and Arab American life.

**BETH GORDON** is a poet, mother, and grandmother currently landlocked in St. Louis. Her poems have been published in numerous journals and her chapbook, *Morning Walk with Dead Possum, Breakfast and Parallel Universe* was published in 2019 by Animal Heart Press. She is also Poetry Editor of *Gone Lawn*.

**PETER GRANDBOIS** is the author of ten books, the most recent of which is *half-burnt* (Spuyten Duyvil, 2019). His poems, stories, and essays have appeared in over one hundred journals. His plays have been performed in St. Louis, Columbus, Los Angeles, and New York. He is the Poetry Editor for *Boulevard* magazine and teaches at Denison University in Ohio. You can find him at www.petergrandbois.com.

**STUART GREENHOUSE** is the author of the poetry chapbook *What Remains* (Poetry Society of America). Poems have most recently appeared or are forthcoming in *Boulevard, Cimarron Review, Massachusetts Review,* and *Oversound,* among other journals.

**ATAR J. HADARI**'s *Songs from Bialik: Selected Poems of H. N. Bialik* (Syracuse University Press) was a finalist for the American Literary Translators' Association Award and his debut collection, *Rembrandt's Bible*, was published by Indigo Dreams in 2013. His PEN Translates award winning *Lives of the Dead: Collected Poems of Hanoch Levin* is just out from Arc Publications. He translates a verse bible column for *MOSAIC* magazine.

**ROBERT HAHN** is a poet, essayist, and translator who has received awards from the National Endowment for the Arts, The MacDowell Foundation, and The Bogliasco Foundation. He lives in Boston's North End with his wife Kathleen Baum.

**MYRONN HARDY** is the author of five books of poems, most recently, *Radioactive Starlings*, published by Princeton University Press. His poems have appeared in *The New York Times Magazine, Ploughshares,* the *Virginia Quarterly Review, Michigan Quarterly Review, Prairie Schooner,* and elsewhere.

**ALBE HARLOW** is a 2019 graduate of Columbia University's MFA Writing Program and a reader for *Harvard Review*. A story of his is published in *Charge Magazine* and an essay of his was recently printed in Princeton University's *Inventory*. New York City is his home.

**ANDREW HEMMERT** is a sixth-generation Floridian living in Kalamazoo, Michigan and Colorado Springs. Recent poems have appeared or are forthcoming in *The Baltimore Review, Bat City Review, Iron Horse Literary Review, North American Review,* and *Washington Square Review*. He earned his MFA from Southern Illinois University Carbondale.

**NATALIE HOMER**'s recent poetry appears in *The Boiler, Berkeley Poetry Review, The Cincinnati Review, Atticus Review, Meridian,* and elsewhere. She received an MFA from West Virginia University and lives in southwestern Pennsylvania.

**ANDREW HOUWEN** is a translator of Japanese poetry. His translation, with Chikako Nihei, of the post-war Japanese poet Tarō Naka's poems appeared in *Modern Poetry in Translation, Shearsman, Cha,* and *Tears in the Fence* before being collected in *Music: Selected Poems*, which was published with Isobar Press in 2018.

**T.R. HUMMER** has published fifteen books of poetry and essays, most recently *After the Afterlife* (Acre Books, 2018). He lives in Cold Spring, New York.

**MICHAEL HURLEY** is from Pittsburgh. His work has appeared in or is forthcoming from *The Cincinnati Review, Sycamore Review, New Delta Review, The Massachusetts Review, Copper Nickel, Mid-American Review, Prairie Schooner, Alaska Quarterly Review, North American Review, FIELD, Crab Orchard Review, Blackbird, Washington Square Review,* and elsewhere. His chapbook, *Wooden Boys*, is available from Seven Kitchens Press.

**JADE HURTER** is the author of the chapbook *Slut Songs* (Hyacinth Girl Press, 2017), and her recent work has appeared in *THRUSH, Passages North, Hunger Mountain, Crab Creek Review,* and elsewhere. She teaches English at the University of New Orleans.

**NORIKO IBARAGI** (1926-2006) was the co-founder and co-editor of the magazine *Kai* ('Oar'). She first came to prominence with her strongly individual political poems during the 1950s. Her poetry collections have sold millions of copies. "Room" is from her 1992 collection, *The Drifting Smell of Coffee from the Dinner Table*.

**MITSUKO INOUE** published poetry for many years in Katué Kitasono's avant-garde *VOU* journal. She lived in Matsue, on the Sea of Japan coast, and worked as a correspondent for *Kyodo News*. Her poetry was included in Kenneth Rexroth and Ikuko Atsumi's anthology, *Women Poets of Japan*, published by New Directions.

**SATOSHI IWAI** was born and lives in Kanagawa, Japan. He writes poems in English and Japanese. His English work has appeared in *The Arkansas International, FLAPPERHOUSE, RHINO, Poetry Is Dead, Small Po[r]tions,* and elsewhere.

**DEVIN KOCH** is a queer poet from Nebraska. He has graduated from Virginia Tech with an MFA, and was a former managing editor of *The New River* and *The Minnesota Review*. His poetry has appeared in *Laurus* and is forthcoming in *Duende*. He is the winner of the Marjorie Stover and Vreeland awards.

**MICHAEL LAUCHLAN** has contributed to many publications, including *New England Review, Virginia Quarterly Review, The North American Review, Valparaiso Poetry Review, Sugar House Review, Louisville Review, Poet Lore,* and *Poetry Ireland Review*. His most recent collection is *Trumbull Ave.* (WSU Press, 2015).

**KABEL MISHKA LIGOT** is from Quezon City in the Philippines. He holds an MFA in poetry from the University of Wisconsin-Madison. His work has appeared in *The Margins, Waxwing,* and other journals. He currently lives in the Midwest, where he works behind the desk at a high school library. kabelmishka.com.

**AMY GONG LIU** is a Chinese-American writer based in the San Francisco Bay Area. Her work has been published in *Hobart, Foglifter, Reality Beach, Cosmonauts Avenue, The Columbia Review,* and others. She thinks too much (or perhaps too little).

**ZAFAR MALIK** is a visual artist, Director of Publications and Dean for Development and University Relations at East-West University in Chicago, and the Managing Editor of East-West University's Center for Policy and Future Studies journal, *East-West Affairs*. He lives in Wilmette, Illinois, and maintains his artist studio at the Noyes Cultural Arts Center in Evanston.

**DIANE K. MARTIN** lives in west Sonoma County, California. Her work has appeared in *RHINO, American Poetry Review, FIELD, Harvard Review, Kenyon Review,* and many other journals and anthologies. Her collection, *Conjugated Visits,* was published by Dream Horse Press. A second collection, *Hue & Cry,* is forthcoming from MadHat Press.

**MICHAEL MARTIN**'s first poetry collection, *Extended Remark: Poems From A Moravian Parking Lot,* was published by Portals Press (New Orleans, 2015). His poems have appeared in a number of publications, including *American Journal of Poetry, New Orleans Review, Berkeley Poetry Review, Carolina Quarterly, Gargoyle, Nine Mile Magazine* and *Chattahoochee Review*. He lives in North Carolina with his wife and kids.

**CHLOE MARTINEZ**'s poems have appeared in publications including *Waxwing, Prairie Schooner, [PANK],* and *The Common*. A Pushcart Prize nominee and semifinalist for the 2018 Perugia Prize, she is Program Coordinator for the Center for Writing and Public Discourse at Claremont McKenna College, as well as Lecturer in Religious Studies. chloeAVmartinez.com.

**TARA McDANIEL** teaches poetry at the Loft Literary Center and community centers around the Twin Cities. Her poetry and critical essays have been featured in *Crab Orchard Review, Cimarron Review, Cutthroat, Third Wednesday, Map Literary Magazine, The Loft Blog,* and elsewhere. She is a graduate of the Bennington Writing Seminars.

**CAMERON McGILL** is a poet and musician from Champaign, Illinois. His poems have appeared in *American Poetry Review, Beloit Poetry Journal, Mid-American Review, Sonora Review,* and elsewhere. His chapbook, *Meridians,* is available from Willow Springs Books. He teaches at Washington State University, where he co-directs the Visiting Writer Series.

**TAYLOR MIGNON** is a poet, translator, amateur critic, and the Editor Emeritus and co-founder of *Tokyo Poetry Journal,* editing the "Japan and the Beats" (vol. 5) and "Butoh and Poetry" (vol. 6) issues. He translated the surrealist poet Torii Shōzō for the collected poetry volume *Bearded Cones & Pleasure Blades.*

**JENNIFER STEWART MILLER** is the author of *A Fox Appears: a biography of a boy in haiku* (2015), and her poems have appeared in *Green Mountains Review, Hayden's Ferry Review, Poet Lore, Sugar House Review,* and other journals. Her chapbook *The Strangers Burial Ground* is forthcoming from Seven Kitchens Press.

**FAISAL MOHYUDDIN** is the author of *The Displaced Children of Displaced Children* (Eyewear, 2018) and *The Riddle of Longing* (Backbone, 2017). He has received an Illinois Arts Council Literary Award, *Prairie Schooner's* Edward Stanley Award, and a Gwendolyn Brooks Poetry Prize. He teaches English at Highland Park High School in Illinois and serves as an educator adviser to Narrative 4.

**A. MOLOTKOV** was born in Russia, moved to the US in 1990 and switched to writing in English in 1993. His poetry collections are *The Catalog of Broken Things, Application of Shadows,* and *Synonyms for Silence.* He co-edits *The Inflectionist Review.* Please visit him at AMolotkov.com.

**ALEX MOUW**'s poetry, nonfiction, and scholarship have appeared in *Colorado Review, West Branch, Ruminate, Christianity and Literature,* and other journals. He lives in St. Louis.

**MARCUS MYERS** lives in Kansas City, where he advises gifted high school students, teaches composition, and edits *Bear Review.* His writing has appeared in or is forthcoming from *The Common, The Cortland Review, Hunger Mountain, The Laurel Review, Mid-American Review, The National Poetry Review, Pleiades, Salt Hill,* and *Typo.*

**NAWAL NADER-FRENCH**'s poems appear in *Fence, Bayou Magazine, Texas Review, TheElephants.net,* and elsewhere. Her manuscript, *A Hemmed Remnant,* was a finalist in the 2018 Ron Sillerman Prize for African Poets by the University of Nebraska Press. She is an adjunct professor in Front Range Community College's Department of English and the founding editor-in-chief of *Inverted Syntax.*

CHRISTOPHER NELSON is the author of *Love Song for the New World*, *Capital City at Midnight*, and *Blue House*, published in the Poetry Society of America's Chapbook Series. He is the founder and editor of Green Linden Press and the journal *Under a Warm Green Linden*. For more information visit christophernelson.info.

MUNIR NIAZI (1928-2006) was a poet and songwriter from Pakistan, best known for his work in Punjabi and Urdu. His many honors include a 1992 Pride of Performance Award as well as the 2005 Sitara-e-Imtiaz (Star of Excellence), presented by the Government of Pakistan and considered one of the nation's highest honors.

JOHN A. NIEVES' poems appear in journals such as: *Crazyhorse, Southern Review, Copper Nickel, North American Review*, and *Poetry Northwest*. His first book, *Curio*, won the Elixir Press Annual Judge's Prize. He's an Associate Professor at Salisbury University.

CHIKAKO NIHEI completed a doctoral thesis on Haruki Murakami at the University of Sydney. She is a lecturer at Yamaguchi University. Her translations with Andrew Houwen of Tarō Naka's poetry appeared in 2018 with Isobar Press. In 2019, Routledge published her first academic monograph, *Haruki Murakami: Storytelling and Productive Distance*.

CALEB NOLEN grew up in Pennsylvania and Maryland. He is currently an MFA candidate at the University of Virginia where he is a Henry Hoyns Fellow. In 2019 he was a Work-Study Scholar at Bread Loaf Writers' Conference and his poems have previously appeared in *Fence* and *Nimrod International Journal*.

JAMES NORCLIFFE, a New Zealand poet, has published ten collections of poetry including *Shadow Play* (Proverse Hong Kong, 2012) and *Dark Days at the Oxygen Café* (VUP, 2016). Recent work has appeared in *Landfall, Spillway, The Cincinnati Review, Salamander, Gargoyle*, and *Flash Fiction International* (Norton, 2015). His latest collection is *Deadpan* (Otago University Press, 2019).

ERIC PANKEY is the author of many collections of poetry. He is the Heritage Chair in Writing at George Mason University.

M. NASORRI PAVONE's poetry has appeared in *River Styx, Sycamore Review, New Letters, The Cortland Review, DMQ Review, Cura, Rise Up Review, Pirene's Fountain, Green Hills Literary Lantern, Poemeleon, Wild Goose Review, The Citron Review*, and elsewhere. She's been anthologized in *Beyond the Lyric Moment* (Tebot Bach, 2014), and has been nominated for Best of the Net and twice for a Pushcart Prize.

MARIELLE PRINCE is poetry editor at *The Rupture*. Her most recent publications include work in *Crab Orchard Review, Four Way Review, Ninth Letter*, and *Poetry Northwest*. She received an MFA from UVA and lives in Charlottesville, Virginia. Her first book manuscript was a 2019 finalist for the National Poetry Series.

**CHARLES RAFFERTY** is the author of *The Smoke of Horses* (BOA Editions, 2017). His poems have appeared in *The New Yorker, O - Oprah Magazine, Gettysburg Review, Southern Review, Prairie Schooner*, and *Ploughshares*. Currently, he directs the MFA program at Albertus Magnus College and teaches at the Westport Writers' Workshop.

**LAURA RING** is the author of *Zenana: Everyday Peace in a Karachi Apartment Building* (Indiana University Press). Her poems have appeared in *Rogue Agent, Rise Up Review*, and *Lunch Ticket*, among other places. A native Vermonter, she lives in Chicago.

**PETER ROBINSON** is an internationally renowned poet, translator and literary critic, winner of the Cheltenham Prize, the John Florio Prize, and two Poetry Book Society Recommendations. Recent publications include a monograph, *The Sound Sense of Poetry* (2018), a poetry collection called *Ravishing Europa* (2019), and *The Constitutionals: A Fiction* (2019).

**LINWOOD RUMNEY** is the author of *Abandoned Earth*, winner of the 17th Annual Gival Press Poetry Award. Poems, nonfiction essays, and translations have appeared in *Ploughshares, Kenyon Review Online, Arts & Letters*, and elsewhere. He lives in Cincinnati and teaches at Union Institute & University.

**NATASHA SAJÉ** is the author of three books of poems, most recently *Vivarium* (Tupelo, 2014), a poetry handbook, *Windows and Doors: A Poet Reads Literary Theory* (Michigan, 2014), and a book of personal essays, *Terroir: Essays on Otherness* (Trinity UP, 2020). She teaches at Westminster College in Salt Lake City and in the Vermont College of Fine Arts MFA in Writing Program. www.natashasaje.com.

**CHRISTOPHER SALERNO** is the author of four books of poems and the editor of Saturnalia Books. His most recent collection is *Sun & Urn*, winner of the Georgia Poetry Prize. Other poems can be found in the *New York Times Magazine, New Republic, American Poetry Review*, and elsewhere. He is a Professor of English at William Peterson University and can be found at csalernopoet.com.

**MARA ADAMITZ SCRUPE** is the author of six award-winning poetry collections. She has won or been shortlisted for Canterbury International Arts Festival Poet of the Year, Narrative Prize, Brighthorse Poetry Book Prize, Grindstone International Competition, Fish Prize, Canberra Vice-Chancellor's Award, and UK National Poetry Competition. She is a marathon runner, an accordionist, and School of Art dean, University of the Arts, Philadelphia.

**MAUREEN SEATON** has authored twenty-one poetry collections, solo and collaborative—recently, *Sweet World* (CavanKerry, 2019) and *Fisher* (Black Lawrence, 2018). Her awards include the Pushcart, Iowa Prize, Audre Lorde Award, NEA, Illinois Arts Council Grant, Society of Midland Authors Award, and two Lammys. She teaches at the University of Miami.

**TSUJI SETSUKO** (1927-1993) was a most uncompromising and dedicated avant-garde photographer in 20th century Japan. She consistently published both her written and photographic poetry in *VOU*, edited by Katué Kitasono, and was a member of *Pan Poésie*. She privately published her journal *O* and over 10 books of stories, written poetry, and visual poetry.

**DONNA SPRUIJT-METZ** is Professor of Psychology at the University of Southern California. Her first career was as a classical flutist. Her poetry has appeared or is forthcoming in publications such as the *Los Angeles Review*, *Copper Nickel*, and *Poetry Northwest*. Her chapbook, *Slippery Surfaces*, was published by Finishing Line Press.

**SETH STEPHANZ** is a gay poet who graduated from the Iowa Writers' Workshop in 2018. He grew up in Kansas and Wisconsin, and his work has appeared or is forthcoming in *Forklift, Ohio* and *Black Warrior Review*. He lives in Iowa City.

**LISA GLUSKIN STONESTREET** is the author of *The Greenhouse* (Frost Place Chapbook Prize) and *Tulips, Water, Ash* (Morse Poetry Prize). Her poems have appeared in *Blackbird*, *Kenyon Review*, *Plume*, and *Zyzzyva*, and online at Poem-a-Day and Poetry Daily. She lives in Portland, where she hosts the reading series Lilla Lit. (lisagluskinstonestreet.com)

**MARCELA SULAK**'s fourth poetry collection, *City of Sky Papers*, and first memoir, *Mouth Full of Seeds*, are forthcoming. She's co-edited *Family Resemblance: An Anthology and Exploration of 8 Hybrid Literary Genres*. Sulak is an NEA translation fellow, and has been long-listed for the PEN Award for Poetry in Translation.

**PAIGE SULLIVAN** completed her MFA at Georgia State University, where she served as poetry editor of *New South*. In addition to essays and book reviews, her poetry has appeared in *Arts & Letters*, *Ninth Letter*, *American Literary Review*, and other journals. She lives and works in Atlanta.

**ELIZABETH SYLVIA** is a writer of poems and other lists who lives with her family in Massachusetts, where she teaches high school English and coaches debate. Elizabeth began submitting poems for publication in 2018; her work has also been featured in *Literary Mama*, *Noctua Review*, and *Off the Coast*.

**ANDREW SZILVASY** teaches Literature outside of Boston, and has poems appearing or forthcoming in *CutBank*, *Smartish Pace*, *Barrow Street*, *Tar River Poetry*, and *The American Journal of Poetry*, among others. He lives in Boston with his wife.

**SHUZO TAKIGUCHI** was a poet, painter, and art critic, and one of the most prominent surrealists in Japan. His first collection of poems is *The Poetic Experiments of Shuzo Takiguchi 1927–1937* (Shinchosha, 1967).

**YUKI TANAKA** holds an MFA in poetry from the Michener Center for Writers, and a PhD in English from Washington University in St. Louis. His chapbook, *Séance in Daylight* (Bull City Press), was the winner of the 2018 Frost Place Chapbook Contest. He teaches at Hosei University, Japan.

**ERIC TRAN** is a resident physician in Asheville, North Carolina. His debut collection, *The Gutter Spread Guide to Prayer*, will be published by Autumn House Press in 2020. He is most recently the author of the chapbook *Revisions* (Sibling Rivalry Press), and his work appears in *The Indiana Review*, *DIAGRAM*, *Black Warrior Review*, and elsewhere.

**LEAH UMANSKY** is the author of *The Barbarous Century*. She earned her MFA in Poetry at Sarah Lawrence College and curates The COUPLET Reading Series in NYC. Her poems can be found in *Poetry*, *Guernica*, *Pleiades*, Poets.Org's *Poem-a-Day*, and *The New York Times*. Her poem is from her new manuscript, *OF TYRANT*.

**ALIA HUSSAIN VANCROWN** has published in journals and magazines in print and online. Her poetry has twice been nominated for the Pushcart Prize. Alia works at the Library of Congress in the Law Division. She currently resides in Maryland. For more, please visit aliahussainvancrown.com and Instagram @aliagoestothelibrary.

**HANNAH VANDERHART** lives in Durham, North Carolina. She has poetry and reviews published and forthcoming in *The Kenyon Review*, *The American Poetry Review*, and *The Adroit Journal*. Her book, *What Pecan Light*, is forthcoming from Bull City Press. She is the Reviews Editor at *EcoTheo Review*. More at: hannahvanderhart.com.

**ANASTASIA VASSOS** lives in Boston. Her work has appeared/is forthcoming in various journals, including *Gravel Mag*, *Haibun Today*, and *Comstock Review*. Anastasia is a reader for *Lily Poetry Review* and a Bread Loaf alumna. "Tinos, August 2012" was named "Poem of The Moment" on *MassPoetry.org*. She is a long-distance cyclist.

**MARK WAGENAAR** is the author of three award-winning poetry collections, including the Saltman Prize-winning *Southern Tongues Leave Us Shining*, from Red Hen Press. His fiction and poetry appear widely, including *The New Yorker*, *Tin House*, *The Southern Review*, *Gulf Coast*, *The Cincinnati Review*, and *River Styx*, among many others. He is a father of two, husband of poet Chelsea Wagenaar, and presently an assistant professor at Valparaiso University.

**CLAIRE WAHMANHOLM** is the author of *Wilder* (winner of the 2018 Lindquist & Vennum Prize for Poetry) and *Redmouth* (Tinderbox Editions, 2019). Her poems have appeared in *32 Poems*, *West Branch*, *The Southeast Review*, and *The Los Angeles Review*, among others. She lives and teaches in the Twin Cities. Find her online at clairewahmanholm.com.

**JESSICA L. WALSH** is the author of the collections *The List of Last Tries* and *How to Break My Neck* as well as two chapbooks. Her work can be found in *The Lily Review*, *Tinderbox*, *Stirring*, and more. She is a professor of English at Harper College in suburban Chicago.

**MIKE WHITE** is the author of two poetry collections, *How to Make a Bird with Two Hands* (Word Works, 2012) and *Addendum to a Miracle* (Waywiser, 2017). His poems have appeared in journals including *The New Republic*, *Poetry*, *Ploughshares*, and *The Yale Review*.

**JOHN SIBLEY WILLIAMS** is the author of *As One Fire Consumes Another* (Orison Poetry Prize), *Skin Memory* (Backwaters Prize), and *Summon* (JuxtaProse Chapbook Prize). A twenty-two-time Pushcart nominee and winner of various awards, John serves as editor of *The Inflectionist Review*, teaches for Literary Arts, and is a poetry agent.

**CAITLIN WILSON** is a current MFA candidate in poetry at Virginia Commonwealth University. She received a 2019 AWP Intro Journals Project award, the 2018 Henrietta Spiegel Creative Writing Award, and a Jiménez-Porter Literary Prize. Her work has appeared or is forthcoming in *ENTROPY*, *Iron Horse Literary Review*, and *Rogue Agent*.

**SHANNON K. WINSTON** has been published in *SWWIM Every Day*, *The Inflectionist Review*, and *The Los Angeles Review*, among other venues. Her work has been nominated for a Pushcart Prize and several times for the Best of the Net. Find her here: shannonkwinston.com.

**JANE ZWART** teaches English at Calvin University, where she also co-directs the Calvin Center for Faith & Writing. Her poems have appeared in *Poetry*, *Rattle*, *Boston Review*, *North American Review*, and *Triquarterly*, as well as in other journals and little magazines.

**MARTHA ZWEIG**'s collections include: *Get Lost* (forthcoming from The National Poetry Review Press); *Monkey Lightning* (Tupelo, 2010); *What Kind* (2003) and *Vinegar Bone* (1999, Wesleyan University Press); and *Powers* (1976, a Vermont Arts Council chapbook). Her work has appeared recently in *Denver Quarterly*, *The Yale Review*, and *Poetry*.

# DONORS

Tony & Beth Adler
Liz Alexander
Catherine J. Allen
Jane Fulton Alt
John Amen
Francisco Aragon
Tom Bachtell
Francesca Bell
Katie Bick
Bonnie Billet
Phillip Bimstein
Jan Bottiglieri
Ann Brandon
Stephen Byrne
Sarah Carson
Robin Chapman
Martha Chiplis & John Dunlevy
Dan Cohen & Micki Sand-Cohen
Laura Cohen
Jo Cohlmeyer & Maggie Edgar
Charles & Donna Dickinson
John & Carol H. Eding
David Eingorn
Joe Eldridge

David & Donna Sue Van Cleaf Fish
Bill & Marilyn Floyd
Jan Frodesen
Diane Glancy
Gail Goepfert
Barbara Goldberg & Benjamin Rhatigan
Richard & Janet Goldberg
Ralph Hamilton
Rev. David & Andrea Handley
Mary Hawley
Michael Horvich
Ann Hudson
David & Rochelle Jones
Lois P. Jones
Hari Bhajan Khalsa
Darlene & Ludwig Krammer
Melissa Lamberton
Michael Landau
Dan & Eve Langton
Michael Lenehan & Mary Williams
Jane Levine & Randy Signor
Dianne & David Lipkin
James & Nancy Litke

Ronald Litke & Judy Sickle
Leah Maines
Mike Matheson
Robert & Margaret McCamant
Lynn Beaman McClure
Beth McDermott
Farlan McFarlan
Donald Meckley & Rose Parisi
Vern Miller
Faisal Mohyuddin
Christopher J. Nelson
Larry Nesper
Pablo Otavalo
Roger Pfingston
James Pike
Joe Pitard
Frances Podulka
Marcia Pradzinski
Michael Pronko
Scott Rabinowitz
Robert Rohm
Eleanor Ronquillo
Ann Roubal
Jenene O. Ravesloot & Thomas W. Roby IV

Carol Sadtler
Jacob Saenz
Martha J. Schut
Maureen Seaton
Vivek Sharma
Paul Sohar
Ann Folwell Stanford
Joannie Stangeland
Linda & George Stevenson
Moira Sullivan
Charles Surber
Joyce Sutphen
Pamela Taylor
Neil Tesser
Herbert K. Tjossem
Angela Narcisco Torres
Nick Valenziano
Ken & Sara Vaux
Valerie Wallace
Marsha Warren
Winona Winkler Wendth
Jay Woolford
Mary K. Young

# New From
# RED HEN PRESS

AVAILABLE ONLINE AT REDHENPRESS.ORG
25% OFF ALL SPRING RELEASES FOR READERS OF *RHINO*

Enter code RHINO20 at checkout to receive 25% off all of the below titles at redhenpress.org.

*Glorious Boy*
a novel by
Aimee Liu
$ 18.95

*Her Sister's Tattoo*
a novel by
Ellen Meeropol
$ 17.95

*Tea by the Sea*
a novel by
Donna Hemans
$ 16.95

*Subduction*
a novel by
Kristen Millares Young
$ 16.95

## ALSO COMING THIS SPRING

*Don't Go Crazy Without Me*, a memoir by Deborah Lott
*Rift Zone*, poetry by Tess Taylor
*The Skin of Meaning*, poetry by Keith Flynn
*Moon Jar*, poetry by Didi Jackson
*Hold Me Tight*, poetry by Jason Schneiderman
*Boy Oh Boy*, short stories by Zachary Doss
*After Rubén*, poetry by Francisco Aragón
*Sugar, Smoke, Song*, short stories by Reema Rajbanshi
*Mostly Water*, a memoir in essays by Mary Odden
*The Way a Line Hallucinates Its Own Linearity*, poetry by Danielle Vogel

## RIDE A RHINO, WIN A CLOUDBANK PRIZE

A $200 prize is awarded for one poem or flash fiction in each issue of Cloudbank.

A $1,000 prize, plus publication, is awarded for a full-length manuscript submitted for the Vern Rutsala Book Contest.

**Visit cloudbankbooks.com**
for contest and submission guidelines.

# Nimrod International Journal

| The *Nimrod* Literary Awards | The Francine Ringold Awards for New Writers |
|---|---|
| **$2,000 & $1,000 Prizes & Publication** | **$500 Prizes & Publication** |
| Prizes include a reading at the Awards Ceremony in Tulsa. Selected finalists and semi-finalists will also be published. | Open **only** to writers with no more than 2 previous publications. Selected finalists will also be published. |
| Poetry: Up to 10 pages<br>Fiction: Up to 7,500 words | Poetry: Up to 5 pages<br>Fiction: Up to 5,000 words |
| Submissions accepted Jan. 1st — Apr. 1st | Submissions accepted May 1st — July 15th |
| **Entry Fee:** $20, includes 1-year subscription | **Entry Fee:** $12, includes Spring/Summer issue |

**Submit by mail or online at nimrodjournal.submittable.com**

Nimrod International Journal
800 S. Tucker Dr.
Tulsa, OK 74104
nimrod@utulsa.edu
www.utulsa.edu/nimrod
nimrodjournal.submittable.com

Subscribe to *Nimrod* for just $18.50 (1 year) or $32.00 (2 years)

# The Antigonish Review

In Print since 1970, now available digitally (PDF) for your devices

## Subscription Rates:

1 – Year Digital    **$30.00**
2 – Year Digital    **$45.00**
1 – Year Printed   **$75.00**
2 – Year Printed  **$140.00**

4 Issues per Year
Digital Copies emailed directly to you

Annual Poetry/Fiction Contests

Order online at www.AntigonishReview.com, or Contact us at tar@stfx.ca

Box 5000, Antigonish, NS  B2G 2W5  (902)867-3962

# Sugar House Review

## 10-Year Anniversary Issue Available Now

Take a sneak peek of our latest and past issues at
**SugarHouseReview.com**

Work from our pages has been included in *Verse Daily*, *Poetry Daily*, and *Pushcart Prize: Best of the Small Presses*, 2015, 2014, 2013, and 2011.

# RHINO Reviews

an online zine of contemporary poetry book reviews

**Over 200 reviews — and growing:**
Monica Sok, *A Nail the Evening Hangs on*
Rick Barot, *The Galleons*
Su Hwang, *Bodega*
Ilya Kaminsky, *Deaf Republic*
Natalie Scenters-Zapico, *Lima :: Limón*
Jericho Brown, *The Tradition*

**and many more!**

{10 to 12 fresh reviews every month}

Send queries to editors@rhinopoetry.org
**rhinopoetry.org/reviews**